When was Anno Domini?

Ormond Edwards

When was Anno Domini?

Dating the Millennium

Floris Books

First published in 1999 by Floris Books
Parts of this book are condensed from the author's
The Time of Christ published in 1986 by Floris Books

British Library CIP Data available

ISBN 0-86315-297-X

Printed in Great Britain
by Cromwell Press, Trowbridge

Contents

Introduction   7
  Scarcity of historical sources   8
  The historical and political background   10
  Jewish priestly and royal powers   14

1. Calendars and Festivals   18
  Days, months and years   19
  Harmonizing the calendar   21
  The Seleucid and Actian eras   23
  Sacred and secular calendars   25
  Jewish festivals   27

2. Herod the Great   34
  Herod and the Jews   36
  The reign of Herod the Great   38
  Herod's coinage   40
  Herod's death   43
  Herod's descendants   47

3. Matthew's Nativity: the Star and the Magi
                                                    51
  The two Messiahs   53
  The arrival of the Magi in Jerusalem   59
  The Star of the Magi   62
  The conjunction of Saturn and Jupiter   63
  The myth of Saturn and Jupiter   66
  Dating the arrival of the Magi   68

4. Luke's Nativity and the Enrolment   71
John the Baptist   72
The enrolment   74
The birth of Jesus   80

5. The Baptism of Jesus   83
The rite of baptism   84
The emergence of John the Baptist   86
The Baptism of Jesus   87
After the Baptism   88

6. The Crucifixion   91
The fifteenth year of Tiberius   91
The length of Jesus' ministry   92
Pontius Pilate   96
The eclipse of the moon   98
Summary   103

Conclusion   105

Appendix   109
References   115
Further reading   120
Index   124

Introduction

Is January 1, 2000, really the first day of a new millennium? Already the debate is under way regarding the accuracy of the arithmetic. For strictly speaking, January 1, 2000 falls two millennia after the beginning of the year 1 BC. However, if we calculate from the beginning of AD 1, the epoch or zero point of the civil Common Era, the first day of the third millennium should fall on January 1, 2001. Which of these — if either — is the true date of the millennium?

It ought to be said straightaway how our convention of dates *Anno Domini* (AD) has come about. The Christian era, assumed to be measured from the year of the birth of Jesus, derives from a calculation by Dionysius Exiguus in AD 525, and was popularized by the Venerable Bede. Our practice of dating *Before Christ* was introduced as late as AD 1669 by G.B. Riccioli (1598–1671), who designated the year before AD 1 as 1 BC.[1] Our historical dating, then, has no year 0.

The ensuing millennium controversy is, of course, more than purely numerical. All hinges on whether or not we actually know when Jesus of Nazareth was born. For those more interested in *what* the new millennium will be commemorating, rather than the correct arithmetic, the true date of the millennium can only be established by reference to the true date of the birth of Jesus. Was Jesus really born in AD 1? How confidently can we rely on the original calculation for establishing the years *Anno Domini?*

Finding reliable answers to these questions is not so sim-
ple. A whole range of difficulties obstruct the researcher.
Long before our current interest in the true date of the new
millennium, there was controversy about the date of the birth
of Christ. Many factors have contributed to this disagreement: the different calendars employed in ancient Palestine;
the strangely dissimilar stories of the Nativity in the gospels
of Luke and Matthew; conflicting prophecies and expectations regarding the coming of a Messiah; not to mention the
differing conclusions drawn from astronomical data.

The following chapters address these issues in an attempt to clear up the confusion which has dogged even
scholarly debate and led to at least one life of Christ being
based entirely on the wrong calendar! We shall examine the
historical sources for the life of Christ, thin though they
are, the biblical accounts themselves, and a variety of clues
that can be gained from analysing the calendars and
coinage of the time. We shall expose some of the errors and
traps that others have fallen into along the way, and hope
thereby to establish as accurately as we can the true date of
the birth of Christ. This will reveal to us, in turn, the true
date of the first day of the third millennium.

Scarcity of historical sources

One of the major mysteries of Christianity is the absence of
Christ from the pages of history. The Herods, Pilate,
Caiaphas, Augustus and Tiberius are chronicled as the
great men of the day, but the greatest among them passes
virtually unnoticed. The Evangelists, by contrast, devote
their whole attention to the central figure with little reference to the public events of the day. Their task was to dis-
close the hidden nature of Jesus, the dimension withheld

from the political historian or reporter, the 'open secret' of his earthly nature. A paucity of dates in the Gospels is, therefore, only part of a more general problem of bridging the gap between Gospel and history.

During the nineteenth century, innumerable attempts were made to write a historical biography of Jesus of Nazareth, stimulating a widespread interest in the chronology of his life. The results have proved to be disappointing, and most scholars have come to the conclusion that there is no historical evidence upon which an adequate life of Jesus could be written. Few, if any, of the chronological assumptions made 'in the quest of the historical Jesus' have stood the test of time.

Outside the New Testament, the earliest mention of Jesus is made by the Jewish historian Josephus. Written towards the end of the first century, his *Jewish Antiquities* contains the following strange words:

> About this time there lived Jesus, a wise man, if indeed one might call him a man. For he was one who wrought surprising feats and was a teacher of such people as accept the truth gladly. He won over many Jews and many of the Greeks. He was the Messiah. When Pilate, upon hearing him accused by men of the highest standing amongst us, had condemned him to be crucified, those who had in the first place come to love him did not give up their affection for him. On the third day he appeared to them restored to life, for the prophets of God had prophesied these and countless other marvellous things about him. And the tribe of the Christians, so called after him, has to this day still not disappeared.[2]

The authenticity of this passage has, however, been disputed. Josephus later records the death of James and this account is more widely accepted. Josephus refers to James as 'the brother of Jesus called the Christ.'[3] It is implied that the historian had already introduced the figure of Jesus, whatever interpolation the earlier passage may contain.

The earliest undisputed passage occurs in Tacitus, the historian of imperial Rome *(c.* AD 55–120), where he states: 'Their originator Christ had been executed in Tiberius' reign by the governor of Judea, Pontius Pilatus.'[4]

The historical and political background

In order to make sense of the civil and religious milieu into which Jesus was born, we first need to review the historical and political background leading up to that time.

Nebuchadnezzar's destruction of Jerusalem in 586 BC led to the deportation of Jews to Babylon — the Babylonian Exile — and signalled the end of the kingdom of Judah of Old Testament times. However, a mere fifty years later the Babylonian empire fell to the Persians who allowed the Jews to return to Judea. Following this, the second Temple was built in Jerusalem which was later enlarged by Herod the Great.

Since the Persian Wars in the first half of the fifth century BC, Greek influence had spread throughout the Orient, aided by bands of Greek mercenaries and merchants, who had been attracted by the comparative wealth of states such as Phoenicia. In the fourth century Alexander the Great's campaign expanded the Greek empire to the East, and by 333 BC the Greeks had occupied Damascus. The battles which ensued from this opening of the Orient to Greek domination were followed by an acceleration of economic life, and the expansion of Hellenistic culture.

On the death of Alexander, his empire was divided among his generals: Ptolemy received Egypt and Seleucus was allotted Syria, including Palestine, although Ptolemy decided to keep the latter for himself. Meanwhile, Jerusalem was still ruled by the High Priests of the family of Onias, who fortified the Temple and improved the city's water supply. Wars were waged between the descendants of Ptolemy and Seleucus, and in 200 BC the contested province was won by Antiochus III of Syria. The Jews helped Antiochus and were rewarded with a charter confirming their ancestral laws, and freeing their leaders fully, and the rest of the people partially, from all taxation.

During the third and fourth centuries BC the Romans were steadily advancing, and ten years after his victorious campaign in Palestine, Antiochus III was defeated in battle by the Roman legions. At the Temple, the High Priest Onias III was dismissed and replaced by his corrupt brother, Jason. However, the Syrians again chose to replace Jason with their own appointee, Menelaus. Jason's attempt to seize Jerusalem gave Antiochus an excuse to send in his troops, who subsequently defiled the altar of the Temple. Menelaus and his followers therefore revolted. A resident priest, Mattathias the Hasmonean, fled with his five sons after slaying two of the King's men. The Hasmoneans rebelled and tore down heathen altars. Mattathias' third son, Judas Maccabeus, took command on the death of his father and continued to rebel against the Seleucids' rule over Palestine.

The Romans, who were keen to damage the Seleucids since they regarded them as the strongest of the eastern Greek states, took up the Jewish cause and made an

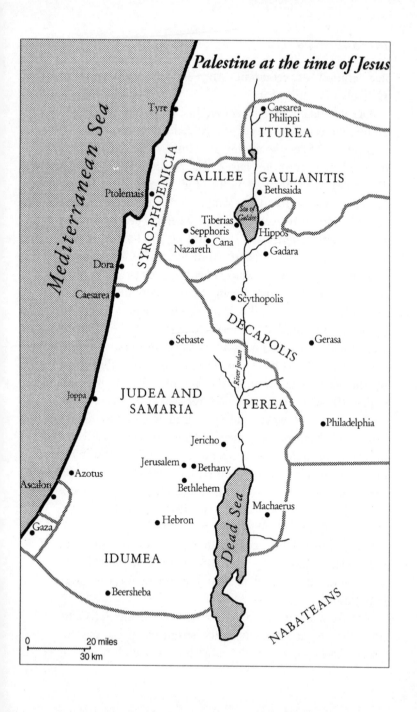

Palestine at the time of Jesus

alliance with Judas Maccabeus. Eventually, the Hasmoneans gained control of large parts of the Seleucid empire. The subsequent period in the Orient was very unstable, which allowed an opportunity for the Roman statesman, Pompey, to intervene between the warring factions of the Hasmonean dynasty. Pompey pronounced in favour of the weaker faction, John Hyrcanus II. His opponent, Aristobulus II tried to resist but was captured by the Romans.

Pompey's settlement of oriental affairs lasted until the assassination of Julius Caesar in 44 BC. The ensuing disruption, stemming from the rivalry of Octavian and Mark Antony, gave the deposed Hasmonean faction an opportunity to recapture their power base. However, they lost the battle and Mark Antony appointed Herod and Phasael as Tetrarchs under the ruling Hyrcanus.

In 40 BC, the Parthians invaded Syria and Judea. Taken prisoner, Phasael committed suicide, and Hyrcanus was mutilated and so rendered unfit to be High Priest. Herod attempted to retaliate but lacked an army. Jerusalem fell and Antigonus was crowned King. Herod fled to Masada, the desert fortress overlooking the Dead Sea, and then to Rome.

There Octavian and Mark Antony appointed him as King — in the Hellenistic sense of conqueror — although Herod, being an Idumean and only half Jewish, was of neither royal nor priestly descent. Indeed, in Jewish eyes, he was a commoner without any legitimate claim to the throne.

On returning to the Orient, Herod launched a campaign to win back the kingdom from Antigonus. His capture of Jerusalem in 37 BC effectively brought Hasmonean rule to an end.

From then on, Herod's position in the Roman Empire depended on his governance of the Jews. His main aim

became to forge links between the Jews and the world
around them.

At the time, then, when Jesus was born, although the region was largely Hellenized and subdued by Roman power,
the religious life remained Jewish and still coloured by
memories of the Jewish exile in Babylon. The influence of
Babylonian culture in Jewish tradition can be traced back
to that bitter period. Herod's response to the religious real-
ities of his time was to appoint malleable men as High
Priests.

Jewish priestly and royal powers

*And the Jews and their priests decided that Simon
should be their leader and High Priest for ever, until
a true prophet should arise ... In recognition of the
Hasmonean family's valiant resistance to Seleucid
persecution, the High Priesthood was conferred on
the brother of Judas Maccabeus in perpetuity.*

(1Macc. 14:25)

At the time of Simon Maccabee's appointment as High
Priest, 'in perpetuity' meant that the office of High Priest
should pass to the house of Hasmon only until this provisional High Priesthood should come to an end with the ap-
pearance of the Messianic prophet. But Simon was not
accorded the royal title. This was withheld pending the
emergence of the royal Messiah. In Judaism prophet,
priest, and king each had clearly defined spiritual roles,
which could not be undertaken by a single individual with-

out corruption unless he were perfect. At intervals during the period of Hasmonean rule, the separation of priestly and royal powers became a vital public issue, as Simon's descendants sought to enhance their personal power and prestige by combining them.

It was this issue which led to a breach between Simon's immediate successor John Hyrcanus (135–104 BC) and the Pharisees, and brought about his alliance with the Sadducees. Hyrcanus on one occasion solicited advice from the Pharisees. After offering the expected praise, one of them added: 'As you wish to know the truth, then know that if you wish to be righteous, lay down the office of High Priest and content yourself with ruling the nation.'[5]

Hyrcanus' subsequent alliance with the Sadducees revealed his worldly aspirations coming to the fore, and a distinct weakening of the Hasmonean's religious interest. On this subject, A. Schalit is well worth quoting at length:

The Pharisees saw in the concentration of the two offices, the kingship and the High Priesthood, in the hands of this dynasty the ominous instrument with which the Hasmoneans were attempting to carry out their designs. Such concentration meant that the Hasmoneans not only conducted the temporal affairs of the nation but —and this the Pharisees considered far more important — they also held the reins of religious affairs, so that they were in a position to mold the nation's religious and moral character in accordance with their secular ambitions.

The Pharisees regarded this state of affairs as intolerable, and they were firm in their resolve to separate the two offices. They insisted that the Hasmoneans content themselves with the monarchy and relinquish the High Priesthood. What was the political significance of this demand? In order to understand this we must recall the Pharisees' view of the role of religion in the life of the Jewish people. The Pharisees regarded religion as the sum and substance of the Jewish people. Religion in their opinion should embrace the nation's life in all its manifestations; in economic affairs and labor, art and thought, law and politics, the life of society and of the individual ... In the eyes of the Pharisees, therefore, the Hasmonean state ... which had blurred the boundaries between Israel and the nations and drawn the Chosen People close to the way of life of the gentiles, had caused it to forget the cardinal fact in its life which had determined its character forever: its existence as a holy people. For this reason the state which the Hasmonean dynasty had founded could not satisfy the yearnings and the hope of the Pharisees. These could be satisfied only by the kingdom of the Messiah of the House of David. That kingdom alone they regarded as the fitting framework for the life of the Chosen People.[6]

The issue of the separation of priestly and royal powers was therefore also reflected in the kind of expectation to be fulfilled by the coming Messiah. The spirit of Messianism, which had been fired by the Maccabean revolt, subsequently underwent many changes. Schürer traces the changes in the older Messianic hope.[7] Its scale grew from national to global redemption. At the same time the extension of hope for the future altered its focus from the people at large to the just individual. And during the first Christian century the Scriptures were searched diligently for illumination on the coming of the Messiah — or several Messianic figures fulfilling royal, priestly and prophetic roles.

We shall see later how closer attention to this older tradition of several Messianic figures helps to clarify the discrepancies that have long puzzled readers of the Nativity narratives in Matthew and Luke.

1. Calendars and Festivals

In examining the time of the birth of Jesus, we are concerned with the earthly life of an individual who was executed in Jerusalem while Pontius Pilate was Roman governor of Judea. Luke's gospel tells us that John the Baptist's ministry began in the fifteenth year of Tiberius Caesar. Against this background, we need some understanding of the political eras and the civil calendar, especially during the Roman period. Just as priestly and civil powers were to be separated in Jewish life, so different political and religious calendars governed events, depending on their nature. We need to explore how and when the calendars were applicable, and, importantly, what were the differences between them.

In examining Gospel chronology we must realize that a number of important events in the Gospels are connected with specific religious festivals, although these are by no means always named. As one instance of this, no New Year festivals are identified as such by the Evangelists, yet it would seem that the Annunciation stories, the beginnings both of the Baptist's ministry and of the Christ's Galilean teaching ministry, as well as the beheading of John the Baptist, all are connected with religious New Year days.

Days, months and years

Great advances have been made with modern instruments in the study of the celestial rhythms. The cyclical movements of sun, moon and stars constitute the time-organism that is an essential part of the earth and of the human, living body. The ancients, too, observed these rhythms with the naked eye and devised calendars from the three fundamental cycles of day, month and year.

In the case of the Jewish calendar, the days of the week were numbered and not named. The months also were numbered (commencing in the spring) but, after the Captivity, Babylonian month-names were also employed.

The day began after sunset when the stars began to appear. This continues to be Jewish religious custom although civil dates are now normally measured from midnight to midnight. For example, Nisan 14, sunset April 2, to sunset April 3, AD 33 is abbreviated to: Nisan 14, April 3, AD 33.

The average time between one new moon and the next is 29.530588 days. Astronomers call this the synodic month. The astronomical new moon is, of course, invisible and the first sickle becomes visible in the evening at least 18 hours later. The Jewish month therefore began with the observation of the first sickle of the new moon, and was thus sometimes 29 days, and sometimes 30 days long. According to the medieval Jewish philosopher, Maimonides (1135–1204):

Just as the astronomers who discern the positions and motions of the stars engage in calculation, so the Jewish court [Sanhedrin], too, used to study and investigate and perform mathematical operations, in

	Jewish	Equivalent	Babylonian
1	Nisan	March/April	Nisanu
2	Iyyar	April/May	Aiaru
3	Sivan	May/June	Simanu
4	Tammuz	June/July	Duzu
5	Ab	July/August	Abu
6	Elul	August/September	Ululu
7	Tishri	September/October	Tashritu
8	Heshvan	October/November	Arahsamnu
9	Kislev	November/December	Kislimu
10	Tebeth	December/January	Tebetu
11	Shebat	January/February	Shabatu
12	Adar	February/March	Addaru
	VeAdar	(intercalated month)	

Table 1. Jewish and Babylonian month names.

order to find out whether or not it would be possible for the new crescent to be visible in its 'proper time,' which is the night of the 30th day. If the members of the court found that the new moon might be visible, they would be obliged to be in attendance at the court house for the whole 30th day and be on the watch for the arrival of witnesses. If witnesses did arrive, they were duly examined and tested, and if their testimony appeared trustworthy, this day was sanctified as New Moon Day. If the new crescent did not appear and no witnesses arrived, this day was counted as the 30th day of the old month.[1]

In the compilation of Jewish law, the Mishnah, we find:

> In Jerusalem there was a special courtyard where the witnesses were examined and entertained ... In the examination of witnesses they were interrogated with such questions as to whether the moon had been seen to the north or to the south of the sun ... Rabbi Gamaliel II even had a diagram of the phases of the moon on a tablet hung on the wall of his upper chamber, and used it in questioning the witnesses.[2]

Harmonizing the calendar

The length of the year is determined by the planetary journey of the earth around the sun. From one spring equinox to the next, the year is, on average, 365.242203 days long. It follows that every year cannot have the same number of days. Our modern year-measurement is based on the Julian calendar — introduced by Julius Caesar in 46 BC — which had standard years of 365 days but a leap year of 366 days every fourth year, giving an average year length of 365.25 days. However, over the centuries this small discrepancy accumulated, and so in 1582, the Gregorian calendar reform was introduced, which leaves out the leap year every hundred years (as in 1900), but adds it every four hundred years (as in 2000).

Ancient calendars used different methods of intercalation (inserting a day or a month) to harmonize the calendar. The Babylonian and Jewish calendar years consisted of 12 lunar months (354 days) with an additional month added every two or three years to keep up with the true year.

In biblical times, there was a difference between Babylonian and Jewish practice in the method of intercalation. In contrast to Babylonian use of the regular intercalation cycle, the Jews retained into the fourth Christian century the empirical method of repeating the last month of the year as necessary to prevent Passover from falling too early.

The Jewish ecclesiastical year was parallel to, but by no means always coincident with, the Babylonian year. Where the Babylonians intercalated a month to prevent their spring New Year's day, Nisannu 1, from falling before the vernal equinox, the Jews intercalated to prevent Passover (Nisan 15) from falling before the same equinox. On average, therefore, the Jewish month began 14 days before its Babylonian namesake; that is, a month earlier nine times in 19 years. Failure to observe this distinction led a highly-regarded American historian of the Near East, A.T. Olmstead, to write a life of Jesus based entirely on the wrong calendar.[3]

Ancient authority for the Jewish empirical style of intercalation is provided by Anatolius (d. AD 282), Bishop of Laodicea who lists his supporting evidence:

> We can learn ... from the statements of Philo,
> Josephus, and Musaeus, and not them only but still
> earlier writers, the two Agathobuli, famous as
> teachers of Aristobulus the Great ... These
> authorities, in explaining the problems of the
> Exodus, state that the Passover ought invariably to
> be sacrificed after the spring equinox, at the middle
> of the first month; and that this occurs when the sun
> is passing through the first sign of the solar, or as
> some of them call it, the zodiacal cycle. Aristobulus
> adds that it is necessary at the Passover Festival that

not only the sun but the moon as well should be passing through an equinoctial sign. There are two of these signs, one in the spring, one in the autumn, diametrically opposite each other, and the day of the Passover is assigned to the fourteenth of the month, after sunset; so the moon will occupy the position diametrically opposite the sun, as we can see when the moon is full; the sun will be in the sign of the spring equinox, the moon inevitably in that of the autumnal.[4]

Modern chronologists have interpreted the passage as an explanation caged in terms (zodiacal cycle) comprehensible to Gentile readers but not faithful to Jewish practice. For example:

There is no evidence that the vernal equinox played any role in this procedure. The statement by Josephus that the Greek month Xanthikos is the same as the Hebrew Nisan, which is the first month of the year when the sun is in Aries ..., provides information for his Hellenistic readers but is not a principle of the Hebrew calendar.[5]

There is, however, strong evidence that the then current Babylonian empirical practice was imposed on Jerusalem in 603 BC and Anatolius simply demonstrates that usage had not changed in the ensuing centuries.[6] The Jews did not adopt the nineteen-year intercalation cycle until the fourth Christian century.

The Seleucid and Actian eras

In ancient times there was no universally recognized numbering of years like our BC/AD system. Historical events were usually fixed by reference to the year of a ruler — as 'in the fifteenth year of Tiberius' — or to the date of a significant event like the Battle of Actium, which provided the starting point for the new Roman era.

Such dating systems sometimes outlasted the life of the ruler. In the case of Alexander's general, Seleucus I, the first historical era began with his occupation of Babylon in 311 BC. When the whole of Syria was granted to him, following the death of Antigonus at the battle of Ipsus in 301 BC, Seleucus inaugurated the Syro-Macedonian calendar, giving Syrian months Macedonian names. After his death, the regnal years of Seleucus continued to be counted as years of the Seleucid era, beginning autumn 312 BC in Syrian reckoning and spring 311 BC in Babylonian/Jewish reckoning. As cities won their independence from the Seleucid kingdom, they dated their years from their independence. Even after Pompey's overthrow of the Seleucids, when events were officially dated by reference to the Roman Emperors (and their precursors), reference to the Seleucid era remained in common use.

Octavian (Caesar Augustus) defeated Antony at the Battle of Actium on September 2, 31 BC, and subsequent events were often dated from this battle, establishing the Actian era (AE) (see Appendix).

Sacred and secular calendars

Judaism bred a profound concern with history which distinguished it from other religions. Other men might worship the revelation of God in nature, but the Jew revered the divine manifestation in the history of his people. Such an emphasis upon the historical Epiphany provided a new element absent in earlier religions.

In his celebrated study *Christ and Time,* Oscar Cullmann distinguishes between 'linear' and 'cyclic' time. Development, evolution and progress emphasize the linear direction of time and this aspect of time is pre-eminent in biblical history. This distinction is valuable in that it highlights the progressive nature of Judaism and Christianity. It would be a mistake to conclude that the cyclic element of time is unimportant. On the contrary, the order of Jewish worship and the path of Christian redemption run through the festival cycle of the sacred year. In the rhythm of the seven-day week, the Mosaic pattern of Creation is ever and again unfolded just as Christianity relives each week the events of Holy Week.

Judaism and Christianity thus both distinguish clearly between the domain of Caesar and the kingdom of God. The Jewish religious calendar was, as already stated, closely modelled on the Babylonian system with its New Year in the spring. Elsewhere west of the Euphrates, Syria and Palestine shared a civil calendar year which began in the autumn. The Syrian calendar differed from its Babylonian counterpart not only in regard to New Year, but also in its unusual practice of adding intercalary months three times every eight years.

After Antiochus III's victory over the Ptolemies at Panias in 200 BC, the contest for Palestine was decided

permanently in favour of the Seleucids. Thereafter Antiochus made the Syro-Macedonian calendar mandatory as
the Palestinian civil calendar, in contradistinction to the
continuing Jewish religious calendar. This civil calendar
was used to record mundane happenings in the departments
of fiscal, military and foreign affairs. As already noted, the
Seleucids had simply translated Syrian month names into
Macedonian Greek.

The Jewish religious calendar has traditionally been
more familiar to us, and in practice biblical scholars have
paid little attention to the Palestinian civil calendar, believ-
ing it to belong rather to the province of Syrian political
history. However, interpretation of Maccabean chronology
requires understanding the relationship between the
Palestinian civil and the Jewish religious calendars and
their use, respectively, of the Syrian and Babylonian
epochs or zero points of the Seleucid era.

Fortunately new data published in 1954 enabled the distinguished biblical scholar J. Schaumberger to clear up
many of the misconceptions and uncertainties.[7] Schaumberger showed that the author of the First Book of the
Maccabees employed two calendars: the Jewish ecclesiastical calendar (with its spring New Year) for all religious
and internal purposes, and the Hellenistic or civil calendar
for all political and external purposes. Ecclesiastical years
ran parallel to the years of the Babylonian Seleucid era and
were likewise numbered from the Babylonian starting-
point spring 311 BC. The essential point is that the civil
year (with its autumn New Year) began some six months
earlier than the equivalent ecclesiastical year. Therefore,
the civil year ran parallel to Antioch's Syro-Macedonian
year which was counted from the Syrian epoch of the
Seleucid era autumn 312 BC. Correct interpretation of a

date, then, requires correct identification of the calendar, whether sacred or secular.

REGNAL YEARS

Civil and military rulers counted the first year of their reign from the autumn (civil) New Year prior to their accession. Thus for instance a ruler coming to the throne in summer 43 BC, would count his first year of rule from the previous autumn 44 BC to autumn 43 BC, so that in effect the first 'year' might be only a few months. It is important to bear this in mind when adding the length of reign of different rulers together, to avoid counting overlapping years twice.

Jewish festivals

The Jewish calendar was marked out by the movement of the moon in relation to the sun. The complement to this movement was the cycle of festivals which were celebrated with a wealth of religious artistry at salient points in the year. Judaism laid upon the devout an obligation to attend whenever possible the three annual pilgrim festivals in Jerusalem. These three feasts were closely associated with harvest celebrations. Firstly, the feast of Unleavened Bread (Passover, Pessach) fell in the spring at the commencement of the barley harvest. Secondly, seven weeks after the beginning of the barley harvest, Harvest or Weeks (Pentecost) was similarly connected with the wheat harvest. Thirdly, in the autumn, Tabernacles or Booths celebrated the ingathering of the year's harvest, and especially of the grape.

PASSOVER

The first month of the ecclesiastical year (Nisan) was the month of Passover and Unleavened Bread. It opened without special ceremony, other than the usual sanctification of the new month by blowing trumpets. On Nisan 10 the sacrificial animals were brought to the Temple (the day of the Cleansing of the Temple). We are told that the day of the Crucifixion was Friday (the day of preparation for the Sabbath, Mark 15:42) and also the eve of the Passover (the day of preparation for the Passover, John 19:14), that is Nisan 14. When Passover fell on the Sabbath — a great and holy day — the daily evening burnt offering was slaughtered at 12.30 pm and offered at 1.30 pm (Friday). The Passover lambs were slaughtered in vast numbers thereafter.[8]

The Feast of Unleavened Bread prescribed a diet of the 'bread of affliction' for seven days after all leaven had been removed. There is no agreement about the precise dates involved, but its beginning was connected with the commencement of the barley harvest. For calendary reasons, the Pharisees insisted that the first sheaf of barley, the omer, was reaped on the day after Passover, that is Nisan 16, whereas the Sadducees and the Samaritans observed the Sunday after Passover for the same purpose. The practices coincided in 33, the year of the Crucifixion.

The Mishnah has a lively account of the cutting of the first barley sheaf:

> The messenger of the court [Sanhedrin] used to
> call out on the eve of the festival and tie the corn
> in bunches while it was yet unreaped to make it
> easier to reap; and the towns near by all assembled

there that it might be reaped with pomp. When it grew dark he called out, 'Is the sun set?' and they answered 'Yea!' 'Is the sun set?' and they answered 'Yea!' 'Is this a sickle?' and they answered 'Yea!'

'Is this a sickle?' and they answered 'Yea!' 'Is this a basket?' and they answered 'Yea!' 'Is this a basket?' and they answered 'Yea!' On the Sabbath he called out 'On this Sabbath?' and they answered 'Yea!' 'On this Sabbath?' and they answered 'Yea!' 'Shall I reap?' and they answered 'Reap!' 'Shall I reap?' and they answered 'Reap!' He used to call out three times for every matter and they answered 'Yea, yea, yea!'[9]

The harvest begun in such impressive style lasted for seven weeks. The Jewish Easter festival provides a perfect example of the way in which the divine gift of human freedom (Passover commemorated the departure from bondage in Egypt) rested on the right relationship between the natural and the spiritual.

PENTECOST

Pentecost also had its agricultural basis. Since it fell seven weeks after the offering of the first barley sheaf, there was disagreement between the Pharisees who observed Sivan 6 and the Sadducees and Samaritans who celebrated Pentecost on the Sunday of Sivan 6–12.

The second of the three feasts is the Feast of Harvest or the Feast of Weeks. Some tables of the festivals prescribe the counting of the full seven

weeks, others only mention the last day, the feast
itself. The seven weeks are counted from the beginning of the barley harvest; the fiftieth day, the Feast
of Harvest, coincides with the end of the wheat
harvest: the first fruits of the wheat harvest are
brought in on this day.[10]

When van Goudoever adds that the wave-offering, the
tenuphah (meaning 'consecration') of two wheat (leav-
ened) loaves, is offered at the Feast of Weeks to the Lord,
he does not really clarify the picture. It is possible that he
intended to state that Harvest coincides with the end of the
barley (not wheat) harvest, since he makes it clear that we
are concerned with the first-fruits of the wheat harvest. But
he goes on to speak again of the end of the harvest being
celebrated at Pentecost.

Perhaps the parallel between Pentecost (after forty-nine
days) and the Jubilee (after forty-nine years) indicates that
the common motif is release. Professor John Gray of
Aberdeen explained to me that Pentecost was a festival offering of first-fruits, thereby deconsecrating the remainder
of the crop so that it became available for the people.

Both Pentecost and Jubilee were a time of revelation
and redemption. Historically, the feast of Pentecost commemorated the giving of the Law on Sinai. Philo indeed,
comes close to the New Testament picture of the festival of
the Holy Spirit, whilst telling of the giving of the Mosaic
Law.

Then from the midst of the fire that streamed from
heaven there sounded forth to their utter amazement
a voice, for the flame became articulate speech in
the language familiar to the audience, and so clearly

and distinctly were the words formed by it that they seemed to see rather than hear them. What I say is vouched for by the law in which it is written, 'All the people saw the voice.'[11]

TABERNACLES

Just as Passover was followed by the opening of the harvest season, the Feast of Booths, Tabernacles or Ingathering celebrated the end of the harvest season. Ingathering was preceded by ten days of prayer and penitence starting at the autumn New Year's day, Tishri 1, and ending Tishri 10, the Day of Atonement (Yom Kippur). On New Year, it is said, God opens three books. The first contains the names of the virtuous and pious, who are inscribed forthwith for life and blessing during the ensuing twelve months. The second contains the names of the irremediably wicked and impious; these are inscribed forthwith for death and disaster. In the third, however, are written the names of the 'betwixt-and-betweens' who are given the chance to determine their own fates by prayer and penitence, for the record is not sealed until twilight on Yom Kippur. After preparation on the Day of Atonement, the High Priest on this day alone entered the Holy of Holies of the Temple. On this single occasion in the year, as the High Priest reached the end of each Scriptural quotation, he uttered the otherwise ineffable name 'Yahweh,' instead of the usual 'Adonai' (Lord).

Like Passover and Pentecost, the autumn festival was an occasion on which ideally all Israelites should make their pilgrimage to Jerusalem. During the summer, the first-fruits had been gathered of grain, wine, oil, honey, and all the produce of the field,[12] while the people lived in trellised-roofed cabins of intertwined branches of olive, myrtle, palm, carob and oleander. And at the autumn full moon they celebrated with great joy the feast of the Jews. They remembered also the time when the people had lived in tents during their forty year wandering in the wilderness when a special tent had served as Tabernacle up to the building of Solomon's Temple. The feast retained the element of Temple dedication.

THE FEAST OF DEDICATION

Lastly, at midwinter, the Feast of Dedication *(Hanukkah)* was celebrated for eight days, beginning on Kislev 25, to commemorate the victory of Judas Maccabeus over the Seleucid tyrant Antiochus Epiphanes (son of Antiochus III), and the subsequent rededication of the Temple in 165 BC. On this day each year, Hanukkah is marked by the lighting of eight lamps at dusk, one lamp being lit on the first evening, two on the second, and so on. Already in Judaism, then, we find a tradition which is echoed in the Christian custom of lights on the Christmas tree.

FASTING DAYS

There were in the sacred year of Judaism additionally four fast days. J. van Goudoever says that the fasts were all associated with the siege and fall of Jerusalem in 586 BC under Nebuchadnezzar.[13] They came into existence during the Babylonian Captivity and were revived after the destruction of the second Temple in AD 70. In which case it is understandable that the destruction of the Temple in AD 70 was mourned after the war with Rome, even though the days were overtly connected with the earlier tragedy.

Tebeth 10	Beginning of the siege	Dec 26
Tammuz 17	Breach of the city walls	June 26
Ab 9	Destruction of the Temple	July 12
Tishri 3	Assassination of Gedaliah	Sep 9

Although it has been rightly emphasized that Judaism and Christianity share the concept of *linear* time, of progress in history, we should not underestimate the role in all religious life of *cyclic* time (see p.25). Redemption is the theme of biblical history and both the order of Jewish worship and the path of Christian redemption run through the festival cycle of the sacred year.

2. Herod the Great

Posterity has acclaimed Herod as 'the Great,' yet nothing more was originally intended by this title than Herod 'the First.' Born into a powerful family which was allied with the dominant world power, Herod enjoyed many advantages as aspirant to the throne — his father, Antipater, a skilled politician, had been confirmed in office as Procurator of Judea by Julius Caesar. Though Herod was a commoner and only half Jewish with no legitimate claim to the throne, as a child his royal future had been foretold:

> There was a certain Essene named Manaemus,
> whose virtue was attested in his whole conduct of
> life and especially in his having from God a
> foreknowledge of the future. This man had (once)
> observed Herod, then still a boy, going to his
> teacher, and greeted him as 'king of the Jews.'
> Thereupon Herod, who thought that the man either
> did not know who he was, or was teasing him,
> reminded him that he was only a private citizen.
> Manaemus, however, gently smiled and slapped him
> on the backside saying, 'Nevertheless, you will be
> king and you will rule the realm happily, for you
> have been found worthy of this by God. And you
> will remember the blows given by Manaemus, so
> that they, too, may be for you a symbol of how
> one's fortune can change. For the best attitude for
> you to take would be to love justice and piety

toward God and mildness toward your citizens. But I know that you will not be such a person, since I understand the whole situation. Now you will be singled out for such good fortune as no other man has had, and you will enjoy eternal glory, but you will forget piety and justice. This, however, cannot escape the notice of God, and at the close of your life His wrath will show that He is mindful of these things.'[1]

Herod's father Antipater was already playing a powerful role as steadfast friend of Rome at the time of Pompey's capture of Jerusalem in 63 BC. This was the long-delayed outcome of the pact with Rome made a hundred years earlier in a moment of despair by Judas Maccabeus. Following his victory, Pompey appointed the Hasmonean (family name of the Maccabean dynasty) John Hyrcanus II as High Priest.

In time, against the unstable background of the situation in Palestine, the value to Rome of Antipater's son was recognized by Julius Caesar and Antony, who made Herod a Tetrarch (a minor prince) in 42 BC.

A Parthian invasion soon thereafter deposed Hyrcanus and installed his nephew Antigonus as High Priest and King in Jerusalem, forcing Herod to flee to his protectors in Rome. Only days earlier, Octavian (later Caesar Augustus) and Antony had ceased their hostilities and renewed their alliance with the Treaty of Brundisium on October 2, 40 BC. Herod's arrival was timely and at Octavian and Antony's instigation the Senate appointed Herod as King of Judea at the end of 40 BC.

After returning to Palestine, Herod vigorously prosecuted his campaign to win the kingdom over the next two

years. With the aid of Antony's subordinates the Parthians
were expelled from Palestine and an assault on Jerusalem
to displace Antigonus commenced in January 37 BC, thwar-
ted by a violent winter storm. Josephus writes:

> When the tempest abated, he advanced upon
> Jerusalem and marched his army up to the walls, it
> being now just three years since he had been
> proclaimed king in Rome.[2]

Herod then laid siege to Jerusalem, pausing only in his
campaign to marry the Maccabean princess Mariamme,
and captured the city in July 37 BC. Clearly Josephus is
here counting Herod's *de jure* years from the ecclesiastical
spring New Year of Nisan 1, 40 BC. Accordingly the fall of
the capital in July would have occurred in Herod's *de jure*
fourth year. As we shall discuss later, this looks like an erroneous simplification on Josephus' part.

Antigonus was captured and led away to await Antony
in Antioch. Meanwhile Herod's claim to the throne was re-
buffed by a population that, though harried and tortured, remained loyal to Antigonus. Now Herod, exercising a
characteristic mix of ruthlessness and cunning, induced
Antony to do away with his rival who, as long as he remained alive, continued to represent Hasmonean rule. This
was the first time that the Romans had executed a king.

Herod and the Jews

With the removal of Antigonus, in a political gesture to the
Jews Herod renounced his claim to have ruled since the beginning of the war and thereby granted an amnesty to his
enemies. He now sought recognition not from 40 BC, but

'from the date when, after putting Antigonus to death, he assumed control of the state.' He obtained recognition by offering his subjects the irresistible concession of restoring the Hasmonean High Priesthood. After installing Antiochus III, Mariamme's younger brother and the last Hasmonean prince, as High Priest, Herod thereby gained a Jewish coronation for himself on Nisan 1, 36 BC.

During his reign Herod undertook a huge construction programme, building palaces and temples throughout the region, culminating in a grandiose transformation of the Temple.

Nonetheless Herod had transgressed deeply against Jewish religious tradition by engineering recognition of himself as king in the Judaistic sense. He had two sons by Mariamme who were educated in Rome. Fearful of their superior blood claim to his throne, Herod summoned to his side Antipater, his son by his first wife Doris. Antipater soon created enough intrigues to convince Herod that his two younger sons were plotting his downfall in conjunction with the Jews. As a result, Herod travelled to Rome to ask Augustus to judge his sons. Augustus attempted to mediate between them but eventually gave Herod discretionary powers over his family affairs and then withdrew from any further political association with him. Subsequently Herod had his two sons killed and carried out many brutal deeds among the alleged allies in the conspiracy.

From this time on, Herod became increasing possessed by insanity and plagued by disease while Antipater continued to turn his father's affections away from the offspring of Herod's other wives. He finally plotted against his father's life, but his plan was discovered when a messenger succumbed to the poison intended for the king.

Antipater was then lured to Jerusalem where Herod ordered his execution.

In the New Testament, we find Herod portrayed as the antithesis of the new humanity embodied in Jesus. Matthew's Gospel relates how the Magi were warned in a dream not to return to Herod, after which the king ordered all children in Bethlehem under the age of two to be massacred. Herod's well recorded mania and fear of losing the throne were combined in this attempt to destroy the awaited royal child.

Among New Testament scholars, interest in Herod centres on the precise dates of his reign and his death and their bearing on the Nativity narratives. The accuracy of Josephus' lengthy accounts does not always seem reliable. But there are useful indications to be gathered from other sources. We begin therefore with an examination of the dating of Herod's reign, with evidence derived from his coinage.

The reign of Herod the Great

When we come to examining the chronology of Herod the Great's reign, it is crucial to decide whether Herod would have been regarded as a Hellenistic or an Israelite king. As High Priests, Herod's predecessors had reckoned their reigns from the spring New Year, but Herod had no such 'Jewish' credentials and was appointed king by the Roman Senate as *their* king. The Romans and Herod himself would undoubtedly have dated the beginning of his reign from the civil autumn New Year 40 BC.

Yet, as quoted above, Josephus states that Herod began his siege of Jerusalem after the winter storms had abated at the end of his third year (in spring 37 BC). Josephus thus antedated Herod's reign to the Jewish ecclesiastical New Year spring of 40 BC as though he were already the legitimate Jewish king from that time.[3]

As a result, Josephus' chronology places the fall of Jerusalem in Herod's fourth year (in July 37 BC), whereas according to Hellenistic reckoning from the civil autumn New Year 40 BC, Jerusalem fell in his third year, 38–37 BC (autumn). That Herod himself applied the Roman reckoning is confirmed by the date he inscribed on his victory coinage, *Year 3*. Herod therefore counted his regnal years from autumn 40 BC. Since Josephus numbered Herod's *de jure* years from spring 40 BC, his Herodian chronology differs initially from Herod's own *de jure* reckoning used in the coin-date by one year.

Herod dated his first coinage from his Roman coronation; yet later seeking legitimacy in Jewish eyes, he abandoned his claim to have reigned since 40 BC and refrained from such un-Jewish practices as dating coins (see below). This wholly uncharacteristic act of self-abnegation in exchange for a Jewish coronation (in 36 BC) changed not only the year but also the New Year involved in reckoning his regnal years from the autumn to the spring New Year. Given that by the civil reckoning his fourth year began autumn 37 BC, his first Jewish year would have begun in spring 36 BC. The autumn New Year corresponded to the following spring New Year, that is, autumn 37 BC is equivalent to spring 36 BC (see Table 2).

Julian date	Civil calendar			Ecclesiastical calendar		
	Seleucid Era	*Herod (civil)*	*Herod's successors*	*Seleucid Era*	*Antigonus*	*Herod (eccles)*
BC 40 spring				272	1	
40 autumn	273	1				
39 spring				273	2	
39 autumn	274	2				
38 spring				274	3	
38 autumn	275	3				
37 spring				275	4	
37 autumn	276	4				
36 spring				276		1
36 autumn	277					
35 spring				277		2
35 autumn	278					
34 spring				278		3
34 autumn	279					
…	…			…		
BC 5 spring				307		32
5 autumn	308					
4 spring				308		33
4 autumn	309					
3 spring				309		34
3 autumn	310		1			
BC 2 spring				310		35

Table 2. Herod's dates.

Herod's coinage

Steeped in the Hellenistic world of political power and an enthusiastic Hellenizer, Herod issued coins which, unlike Hasmonean and earlier Jewish coins, were dated. The innovation was Hellenistic. In contrast, Herod's Hasmonean predecessor, Mattathias Antigonus, issued *undated* coins which also recorded the proper distinction between the Jewish High Priestly office and the Hellenistic royal office. One coin has in Hebrew on the obverse (main side): 'Mattathias the High Priest and congregation of the Jews,' and on the reverse, 'King Antigonus' in Greek.[4]

As observed above, Herod's first coins were dated *Year 3,* and must have been minted in great abundance as they replaced the entire Hasmonean currency. It is then hardly surprising to find one year's issue exhibiting no less than four coin types. Their issue began after Herod's victory in July 37 BC, and continued after the end of his third year until his Jewish coronation six months later. Afterwards, he did not issue any coins dated *Year 4,* or any other dated coins. The Israel Museum coin specialist, Y. Meshorer, comments on the dated coins:

> It must have been of decisive importance, as otherwise this date, and this one alone, would not have been emphasized to such an extent. Which was the third year of Herod's reign and what happened then?
>
> ... For three years Herod waged war against Antigonus until in 37 BCE he conquered Jerusalem and became the effective ruler of Judea. Hence, what was theoretically his third year was actually his first. The most important event in the early years was undoubtedly his victory over Antigonus and the final overthrow of the Hasmonean dynasty, a victory that was also perpetuated by the minting of a large number of coins to replace those issued by Antigonus during the years when Herod was already the theoretical ruler of Judea.[5]

This interpretation of the coin dating seems at first sight not to be compatible with Josephus' reckoning in *Jewish War*. According to the historian, Herod's accession was antedated officially to spring 40 BC and the siege began at the end of the third year. His victory coin should then have been dated *Year 4*. However, Herod's initial claim to the throne was Hellenistic not Jewish and he would undoubtedly have used the civil calendar, dating his early reign in autumn-to-autumn years starting from autumn 40 BC. It seems that Josephus oversimplified the chronology at this point, sparing his Roman readers the intricacies of the Jewish distinction between the sacred and the profane, the priestly and the royal. As we know from the Seleucid era, the autumn-to-autumn civil year was equated with the spring-to-spring religious year which began six months later. Accordingly Herod's reign began as follows:

Roman Count	Jewish Count	Roman Reckoning	Jewish Reckoning
Herod 1		autumn 40–39 BC	
Herod 2		autumn 39–38 BC	
Herod 3		autumn 38–37 BC	
(Herod 4)	Herod 1	autumn 37–36 BC	spring 36–35 BC

The later *Year 5* coin of Herod Agrippa reveals a similar discrepancy between Josephus' Herodian chronology and Hellenistic usage. Its image of Caligula (Gaius Caesar) ostensibly appears in AD 41–42 (spring), three months after the emperor's death on January 24, AD 41. The anomaly of Gaius' head appearing on a coin after his death strongly indicates that the usual dating of the reign of Herod Agrippa from spring AD 37 is absolutely impossible, particularly when we remember that Gaius' memory was execrated.'[6] The absurdity disappears when Agrippa's reign is dated from the corresponding civil New Year, autumn AD 36, with the issue of the coin actually falling in AD 40–41 (autumn), ten months before Caligula's death.

Herod's coin dated *Year 3* and Agrippa's coin dated *Year 5* show that the same calendary rule operating previously under the Seleucids continued unchanged into the Roman period. It follows that if Herod I dated his *Year 3* coin according to the same Hellenistic calendar as Herod Agrippa's *Year 5* coin, then *Antiquities'* date of Herod the Great's death (spring 4 BC) also has to be rejected.

Herod's death

A growing number of serious studies all conclude that Herod died early in 1 BC.[7] It is not possible, however, to reconcile the coin evidence supporting this conclusion with the accounts of the nearly contemporary historian Josephus unless the calendars are properly understood. Josephus has to compute Herod's reign as 37 years by the Roman count but 34 years as acknowledged by the Jews. Thus, the king died in his thirty-eighth year and thirty-fifth year respectively. Then the final years of the reign are:

(Herod 37)	Herod 34	(autumn 3–2 BC)	spring 3–2 BC
(Herod 38)	Herod 35		spring 2–1 BC

Josephus' statement that Herod reigned for thirty-four years is confirmed in *The Assumption of Moses:*

> There shall be raised up unto them kings [the Maccabees] bearing rule, and they shall call themselves priests of the Most High God; they shall assuredly work iniquity in the holy of Holies. And an insolent king [Herod I] shall succeed them, who will not be of the race of priests, a man bold and shameless, and he shall judge them as they shall deserve. And he shall cut off their chief men with the sword, and shall destroy them in secret places, so that no one may know where their bodies are. He shall slay the old and the young, and he shall not spare. The fear of him shall be bitter unto them in their land. And he shall execute judgments on them as the Egyptians executed upon them, during thirty and four years, and he shall punish them. And he shall beget children, who succeeding him shall rule for shorter periods [Herod's sons are to reign for shorter periods and this incorrect prophecy must have been written before AD 30]. Into their parts cohorts and a powerful king [Varus] of the west shall come, who shall conquer them: and he shall take captive, and burn a part of their temple with fire, and shall crucify some around their colony.[8]

Characteristically, a Jewish source omits the Roman reckoning of Herod's thirty-seven years in favour of the Jewish thirty-four years counted from a spring New Year's day (reckoned as Nisan 1, 36 BC).

It was recounted above that in 37 BC the victorious King

Herod I forced his recognition as a legitimate king in the Jewish sense and that he dated his reign as King of the Jews from spring 36 BC. By this calculation his death 34 years later was in the year 2–1 BC (spring), and the official Jewish date of his death was accordingly antedated to spring 2 BC. His sons won no comparable Jewish recognition and dated their reigns from the equivalent New Year in the civil calendar, autumn 3 BC.

Josephus believed when writing *Jewish War* that Herod died in 3 BC. When he came to write *Antiquities*[9] it must have become clear to him that the chronology of *War* was erroneous, as he discovered that just before Herod died there had been an eclipse of the moon. But no such eclipse had been visible in spring 3 (or 2) BC.[10] Based on the astronomical data, Herod's death had to be placed shortly after the partial eclipse of the moon of March 13, 4 BC or, alternatively, following the total eclipse of January 10, 1 BC. Josephus had to alter his later chronology to take account of this information.

Table 2 (page 40) shows that, calculating from Herod's Jewish coronation on Nisan 1, 36 BC, and following a reign of thirty-four years, Herod died in his thirty-fifth year (spring 2/spring 1 BC). The date can be defined more narrowly by placing his death between the lunar eclipse of January 10, 1 BC and the following Passover on Nisan 15, April 10, 1 BC.[11]

It is possible to state Herod's death date still more precisely, although not with the same degree of certainty. Shortly before his death the hated tyrant had the self-knowledge to realize that the Jews will keep a festival upon my death.' In a fit of megalomaniac depravity he devised a plan:

He got together the most illustrious men of the
whole Jewish nation, out of every village, into a
place [in Jericho] called the Hippodrome, and there
shut them in. He called for his sister Salome, and
her husband Alexis, and made his speech to them: I
know well enough the Jews will keep a festival upon
my death; however, it is in my power to be mourned
for on other accounts, and to have a splendid
funeral, if you will be but subservient to my
commands. Do you but take care to send soldiers to
encompass these men that are now in custody, and
slay them immediately upon my death, and then all
Judea, and every family of them, will weep at it
whether they will or no.'[12]

Though when Herod died, Salome did not carry out this
plan, it is likely nevertheless that Herod's death became a
festival. The *Megillah Taanith* (written after AD 70) mentions two festive days on which fasting was forbidden,
without mentioning the occasions they commemorated:
Kislev 7 and Shebat 2. In the spring-to-spring year 2–1 BC,
only Shebat 2 (January 28, 1 BC) falls after the eclipse.[13]

When calendar, coinage and astronomical data are taken
into account, we have to conclude that Herod died early in
1 BC, soon after the lunar eclipse mentioned by Josephus,
and probably on Shebat 2, January 28, 1 BC.

Following from this, we need to take a fresh look at the
dates of the Nativity narratives in Matthew and Luke. We
begin with Matthew in the following chapter. But as their
names figure in the political background, it will be useful
to include a few details first on the rulers who succeeded
Herod.

Herod's descendants

After Herod the Great's death his kingdom was divided by Caesar Augustus and passed on to his sons. Josephus' treatment of these is slight compared with his coverage of Herod's own reign:

> But although the history of Herod is treated in great detail, that of his immediate successors is thin. It almost seems as though Josephus had no written sources to turn to here. The narrative does not fill out again until the reign of Agrippa I (AD 41–44).[14]

ARCHELAUS

Archelaus was the oldest surviving son of Herod the Great, and is mentioned in the Gospels as governing Judea on Mary and Joseph's return from Egypt. On taking possession of his ethnarchy, he did not forget old feuds, and treated not only the Jews but also the Samaritans with great brutality. Both parties denounced him and sent deputations to Augustus, and in the ninth year of his rule, in AD 5–6, Archelaus was deposed and banished to Vienne, a town in Gaul, and his property confiscated to the imperial treasury. He died there ten years later.

ANTIPAS

The second surviving son of Herod the Great, Antipas was Tetrarch of Galilee and Perea. Like his father, Antipas was astute, ambitious and an extravagant builder, constructing the town of Tiberius on the coast of the Sea of Galilee. He married Herodias, the wife of his half-brother Philip. Later,

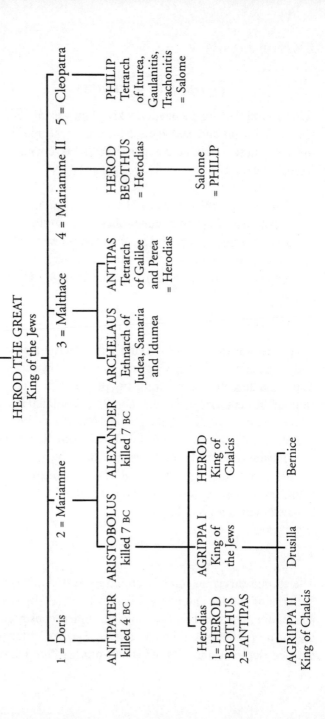

John the Baptist's denunciation of this marriage resulted in the Baptist's imprisonment and his execution as described in the Gospels (Matt.14:3–12, Mark 6:17–29). Josephus reports Herod Antipas' exile, and his kingdom passed to Herod the Great's grandson, Agrippa I.[15]

PHILIP

Herod Philip ruled over Trachonitis, the same largely non-Jewish tetrarchy where Agrippa later became king. Philip, the youngest of Herod the Great's surviving sons, married his niece, Salome, the daughter of Herodias.

According to modern editions of Josephus, Herod Philip reigned from spring 4 BC and died after a reign of thirty-seven years in the *twentieth* year of Tiberius. However, the earlier manuscripts of Josephus in the British Museum and in the Library of Congress say that Philip reigned for 37 years and died in the *twenty-second* year of Tiberius.[16] This again points to 1 BC being the first year of reign, and thus the year of the death of Herod.

AGRIPPA I

After the death of Tiberius, Gaius Caesar appointed Herod's grandson, Agrippa, as king of the tetrarchy of Philip, and on Antipas' exile Agrippa also received Galilee and Perea. Later, he also attained sovereignty of Judea, Samaria and Idumaea, thus controlling the whole of what had been the kingdom of his grandfather, Herod the Great. Luke's Gospel records Agrippa as one of the instigators of the persecution of the Christian Church. After Agrippa had been proclaimed a god in Caesarea he endured a hideous death, following five days of agonizing stomach pains. He is acknowledged by Josephus to have been the last great Jewish monarch in the tradition of Herod the Great.

An important step was taken in understanding the chronology of Herod's early regnal years with the realization that his grandson, the first successor to be crowned — Herod Agrippa — dated his coins according to the civil calendar. Agrippa's numismatic practice must have been previously employed by Philip. His coins bore no Jewish symbols and he was the first Jewish ruler to depict his own portrait on his currency, as well as that of the Roman Emperor. Dr A. Burnett, Keeper of Coins and Medals at the British Museum gives his view on this point:

> An awareness of the importance of Agrippa and his personal relations with two Emperors, and an appreciation of the religious make up of his kingdom, are essential to the example of his coinage ... The regnal years in question are ... civil years starting in the autumn and not religious years starting in the spring.[17]

AGRIPPA II

Agrippa II was the son of Agrippa I and great-grandson of Herod the Great. It is before this ruler that the apostle Paul was brought at the request of Festus before being sent to Rome. The story of how Paul conducted himself before Agrippa is told at length by Luke in Acts 25 and 26.

After the destruction of Jerusalem, Agrippa later in Rome supervised chapter by chapter the writing of Josephus' *Jewish War.*

3. Matthew's Nativity: the Star and the Magi

There was a persistent expectation in Judaism of two Messiahs — one royal, one priestly — and a Messianic Prophet. This expectation is not made explicit in the Gospels. Yet the divergence between the birth narratives in Matthew and Luke is so great that we need to ask whether one of the accounts may not relate specifically and solely to a royal forerunner of the Messiah, the anticipated king of the line of David? Could this explain the differences between the Nativity stories?

In Matthew's Gospel Jesus' family is domiciled in Bethlehem until the flight into Egypt, and Nazareth is mentioned for the first time on their return from Egypt. In Luke's Nativity, the family is forced by the enrolment to travel from Nazareth at the time of the birth. After the birth of the Lucan child, the family does not flee to Egypt but visits the Temple in Jerusalem before continuing on the homeward journey to Nazareth.

King Herod, the Magi and the star shining over the house in Bethlehem, with the journey into Egypt, furnish Matthew's account with its characteristic details, just as the enrolment and the shepherds coming to the stable are features of Luke's Nativity.

There seems to be a clear choice between either (a) rejecting one or both of the infancy Gospels as unhistorical, or (b) accepting both narratives as historical. In the latter

Now when Jesus was born in Bethlehem of Judea in the days of Herod the king, behold, wise men from the East came to Jerusalem, saying, 'Where is he who has been born king of the Jews? For we have seen his star in the East, and have come to worship him.' When Herod the king heard this, he was troubled, and all Jerusalem with him; and assembling all the chief priests and scribes of the people, he inquired of them where the Christ was to be born. 'In Bethlehem of Judea; for so it is written by the prophet:

"And you, O Bethlehem, in the land of Judah,
are by no means least among the rulers of Judah;
for from you shall come a ruler,
who will govern my people Israel."'

Then Herod summoned the wise men secretly and ascertained from them what time the star appeared; and he sent them to Bethlehem, saying, 'Go and search diligently for the child, and when you have found him, bring me word that I too may come and worship him.'

When they had heard the king, they went on their way; and lo, the star which they had seen in the East went before them, till it came to rest over the place where the child was. When they saw the star, they rejoiced exceedingly with great joy; and going into the house they saw the child with Mary his mother, and they fell down and worshipped him. Then, opening their treasures, they offered him gifts, gold, frankincense and myrrh. And being warned in a dream not to return to Herod, they departed to their own country by another way.   (Matt.2:1–12)

case, we should then consider whether the solution to the mystery of the Nativity stories may not lie within the Essene expectation of more than one Messianic figure.

The two Messiahs

An invitation to explore the Nativity accounts afresh was presented by the discovery of the Dead Sea Scrolls at Qumran in 1947, in effect a religious library of the Jewish Essene community. These writings confirm the pre-Christian expectation of not one but two Messiahs — one royal, the other priestly — and a Prophet.

The Scrolls mention a companion royal figure who would defer to the priestly Messiah at the Messianic banquet,' and the Nativity of Matthew unmistakably relates the birth of a royal Messiah. Matthew's princely Immanuel of Bethlehem would then equate with the transient but historically real figure of a royal forerunner to the priestly Messiah. John the Baptist would represent the one whose annunciation and birth fulfil the expectation of a Prophet. Jesus of Nazareth (whose birth is recorded by Luke) would equate with the priestly Messiah. Indeed, quite independently of the Scrolls research a German scholar, G. Friedrich[1] came to the unexpected but convincing view that Jesus of Nazareth answered to the expectation of the Messianic High Priest (see below, p.57).

Quotation in the New Testament of Messianic prophecies from the Old Testament should not confuse the reader. These Messianic connotations were for the most part recognized only after the Resurrection. How alien these interpretations were to contemporary Judaism is attested by the behaviour of both the disciples and the opponents of Jesus (for example, their reactions to references to Christ's death and resurrection).[2] There is no evidence that a suffering Messiah was expected.

During the first Christian century the Scriptures were closely explored for textual references to the coming of the Messiah, or several Messianic figures. The spirit of Messianism was intrinsic to Judaism and found full expression in the Maccabean revolt (166–164 BC) with its vision of a true prophet to come (1Mac.14:41), and the appointment of a provisional High Priesthood drawn from the Maccabean (Hasmonean) line. The hope of resurrection raised in the Second Book of the Maccabees marks an important development, and the Book of Daniel, thought to have been written during the Maccabean uprising (second century BC), also proved vastly influential in shaping Messianic expectations.

The figure of the Messianic king is encountered in fuller colour and sharper outline in the Psalms of Solomon, composed most likely in the time of Pompey (63–48 BC). The poet's longing for the Davidic king is particularly vivid because Jerusalem in his time had fallen under the gentile rule of the Romans and no future expectation could be built on the dynasty of the Hasmoneans. He therefore hopes that God will raise up a king from the line of David to rule over Israel.[3] There is also evidence of Messianism during the reign of Herod the Great in Josephus.[4]

The Assumption of Moses, an apocryphal work dating from around the beginning of the Christian era, prophesies in beautiful and spirited language the advent of the spirit of God:

> And then his kingdom shall appear among all
> creatures. And then Satan shall be no more and
> sorrow shall depart with him ... For the Heavenly

One shall arise from the throne of his kingdom, and
he shall go forth from his holy dwelling-place with
indignation and wrath for his children's sake. And
the earth shall tremble; to its ends shall it be shaken;
and the high mountains shall be brought low and the
hills shaken ... shall change into blood (compare
Joel 3:4), and the circle of the stars shall fall into
disorder ...[5]

It is unlikely to have escaped the Herodians that Virgil's
Fourth Eclogue was composed at the time of Herod's coronation in Rome. The occasion which prompted the poet
was the temporary reconciliation between Octavian
(Augustus) and Antony following the Treaty of Brundisium
on October 2, 40 BC. In his celebration of the event Virgil
mentions the anticipated birth of a special child:

Now there has come the last age of which the
Cumaean Sybil sang; a great orderly line of
centuries begins anew; now too the Virgin returns;
the reign of Saturn returns; a new generation
descends from the high heavens. Upon the Child
now to be born, under whom the race of iron will
cease and a golden race will spring up over the
whole world ...[6]

As we saw earlier the Essene Order awaited both the
Prophet and the Davidic King as forerunners of the priestly
Messiah who would take precedence over them. The
Prophet is mentioned explicitly only once: they [the members of the Community] shall depart from none of the
counsels of the Law ... until the coming of the Prophet and
the Messiahs of Aaron and Israel.'[7]

The Scrolls describe the Messianic banquet to be held when God would beget the Messiah to be present among them.[8] The Priest will be accompanied by the Sons of Aaron, and the Messiah of Israel — as military commander — by his commanders. The *Priestly* takes precedence over the *Davidic* Messiah in all spiritual matters. Karl Georg Kuhn explains:

> The concept of the two Messiahs, a priestly and a political one, is actually not as strange as it first appears to be. The entire structure of post-exilic Israel shows the side-by-side position of the priestly hierarchy and a worldly political leader-ship. This structure is given already in the juxta-position of the priests and the princes' as worldly leaders, found in Ezekiel 44–46. In Zech.4:14 *(c.* 520 BC) we see, side-by-side, the Aaronite Joshua, the High Priest, and the Davidic Zerub-babel, the worldly leader of the Israelite com-munity, as the two anointed ones.' In the final stage of development, more than 500 years later, during the second Jewish insurrection against the Romans (AD 132–135), the same juxtaposition occurs. The High Priest Eleazar stands side by side with the political Messianic leader of the uprising, Simon ben Kosba (bar Kokba). Here, however, contrary to the Essene order of precedence, the political head has the first place, while the High Priest ranks second.[9]

It is not difficult to see that Matthew's Nativity account corresponds to the expectation of a royal Messiah. It is the priestly Messiah who seems to be absent from the

Gospels, although the Christ is portrayed as High Priest in the Letter to the Hebrews and, less explicitly, in the Book of Revelation. After a thorough re-examination of the question, G. Friedrich comes to an entirely different conclusion.[10] He finds that the priestly concept is central to the Gospel picture of Jesus, even though it is not spelled out:

> Every period has its problems and its tasks. Earlier, Jesus had been seen first as Messiah, then as Son of Man, finally as Servant of God. The newly discovered Scrolls prompt an investigation of High Priestly Christology in the Synoptics.

He goes on to say he believes that originally Jesus was regarded and revered exclusively as the High Priest.'

In medieval Judaism we also find the rabbinic doctrine of two Messiahs. Through a better understanding of Jewish Messianism, we are able to examine afresh the great divergences between Matthew's and Luke's Nativity accounts. The complete separation of the three Messianic offices was a prerequisite of the opening of the Messianic age. Only then could they be combined in one incorruptible individual. Later, Christian writers looked back upon the Incarnation as the investment of Jesus with the three Messianic offices. The theologian and church historian Eusebius of Caesarea regards all the High Priests, kings and prophets of the Old Testament as foreshadowing the anointed one:

> Christs in image ... they all stand in relation to the true Christ, the divine and heavenly Word who is the sole High Priest of the universe, the sole King of all

creation, and of prophets the sole Archprophet of the Father.[11]

So, how does the tradition of the two Messiahs resolve itself in the context of one Jesus that died on the Cross? Rudolf Steiner, the founder of anthroposophy, developed an explanation based on the fundamental differences of Matthew and Luke's accounts of the Nativity stories.[12]

The two Nativity stories reveal two different children in terms of background, lineage and temperament. Matthew's Joseph was of royal descent, and lived in Bethlehem. This family fled to Egypt to escape Herod's massacre. Jesus Immanuel was a spirited child with a profound, inherent wisdom. The child of Luke's Gospel was the only child of Joseph of Nazareth, and was born in Bethlehem because of the census, and went back to Nazareth soon after the birth.

After returning from Egypt Matthew's family settled in Nazareth where Luke's family already lived, and the two families became friends. When Luke's Jesus was in his twelfth year, his parents took him to the Temple in Jerusalem. In Luke's Gospel we read how Jesus went missing for three days and his parents finally found him conversing with the teachers in the Temple (Luke 2:41–51). This is the child who had previously been quiet and of a deeply inward nature. It is as if the spirit of Matthew's Jesus has transferred itself to the younger child, thus uniting both the royal and the priestly roles. The royal child of Matthew's Gospel soon dies, leaving the other to fulfil his divine destiny. It is Luke's Jesus who goes on to be recognized and baptized by John, and thus gathering in one person the three roles of priest, king and prophet, fulfils his public ministry and undergoes trial and death on the Cross.

The arrival of the Magi in Jerusalem

Details in Matthew's account of the Nativity allow us various points of historical reference. The first is offered by the following: When Herod the king heard this, he was troubled, and all Jerusalem with him ...' (Matt.2:3)

Compare Josephus' account of the days leading up to the lunar eclipse on January 10, 1 BC. This is the only eclipse mentioned by Josephus and it occurred at the termination of a vigorous disturbance in the Temple:

> Judas, the son of Sariphaeus, and Matthias, the son of Margalothus, were most learned of the Jews and unrivalled interpreters of the ancestral laws, and men especially dear to the people because they educated the youth, for all those who made an effort to acquire virtue used to spend time with them day after day. When these scholars learned that the king's illness could not be cured, they aroused the youth by telling them that they should pull down all the works built by the king in violation of the laws of their fathers and so obtain from the Law the reward of their pious efforts. It was indeed because of his audacity in making these things in disregard of the Law's provisions, they said, that all those misfortunes, with which he had become familiar to a degree uncommon among mankind, had happened to him, in particular his illness. Now Herod had set about doing certain things that were contrary to the Law, and for these he had been reproached by Judas and Matthias and their followers. For the king had erected over the great gate of the Temple, as a votive offering and at great cost, a great golden eagle,

although the Law forbids those who propose to live
in accordance with it to think of setting up images
or to make dedications of (the likeness of) any living
creatures. So these scholars ordered (their disciples)
to pull the eagle down, saying that even if there
should be some danger of their being doomed to
death, still to those who are about to die for the
preservation and safeguarding of their fathers' way
of life the virtue acquired by them in death would
seem far more advantageous than the pleasure of
living ...

With such words, then, did they stir the youth,
and when a rumour reached them that the king had
died, it only made the scholars' words more
effective. At mid-day, therefore, the youths went up
(to the roof of the Temple) and pulled down the
eagle and cut it up with axes before the many
people who were gathered in the Temple ... [Forty
of the young men were speedily arrested and
brought before Herod.] Thereupon the king had
them bound and sent to Jericho where he summoned the Jewish officials, and when they arrived,
he assembled them and lying on a couch because of
his inability to stand, he recounted his strenuous
efforts on their behalf, and told them at what great
expense to himself he had constructed the Temple,
whereas the Hasmoneans had been unable to do
anything so great for the honour of God in the one
hundred and twenty-five years of their reign ...
this was supposedly an insult to him, but in actual
fact, if one closely examined their actions, was
sacrilege.

... Herod ... dealt rather mildly with [them] but

removed the High Priest Matthias from his priestly office as being partly to blame for what had happened ... As for the other Matthias, who had stirred up the sedition, he burnt him alive along with some of his companions. And on that same night there was an eclipse of the moon.[13]

Could Matthew and Josephus have been referring to the same event in Jerusalem? Since the insurrection described by Josephus ended before the lunar eclipse of January 10, 1 BC, which heralded Herod's death, then the disturbance evidently occurred around the time (January 6) traditionally associated with the adoration of the Magi. Writing in 1880, Florian Riess identified the sedition' with the arrival of the Magi which so troubled' Jerusalem. If we accept his conclusion, we have a latest possible date for the Matthean Nativity.

Writing in about AD 194, Clement of Alexandria already confirms the Nativity date handed down by tradition:

From the birth of Christ, therefore, to the death of Commodus [December 31, AD 192] are, in all, a hundred and ninety-four years, one month [30 days], thirteen days. And there are those who have determined not only the year of our Lord's birth, but also the day; and they say that it took place in the twenty-eighth year of Augustus [August 29, 3 BC to August 28, 2 BC on the Egyptian reckoning], and in the twenty-fifth day of Pachon [May 20 (Clement also mentions Tybi 15, January 10, and Tybi 11, January 6)].[14]

Holzmeister[15] interprets Clement's implied date of the

Nativity as November, 3 BC. But K. Ferrari d'Occhieppo is
no doubt correct in assuming that Clement here employs
194 Egyptian years of 365 days without leap years.[16] Then
Clement's assumed year and date of the Nativity is January
6, 2 BC.

Clearly this traditional date of the Nativity on January 6,
relates to Matthew's birth narrative since the date is linked
to the adoration of the Magi, and therefore falls in Herod's
lifetime. Herod was startled at the news of the Magi because his highly efficient intelligence system would have
been expected to have reported anything so untoward as the
birth of a possible Davidic pretender to the throne. If the
child was only newly born at the time of the Magi's visit,
this consternation is comprehensible. The Massacre of the
Innocents would then have coincided with the uprising in
the Temple.

From the evidence of the lunar eclipse, we can agree as
to month and day with the date of the Matthean Nativity in
Eastern tradition, namely, Tebeth 9 (January 6). However
from the same evidence the year must be 1 BC, rather than
Clement's 2 BC.

The Star of the Magi

Determining the nature and timing of the star of Bethlehem belongs to the elucidation of Matthew's birth story.
Among scholars who have specialized in the subject, opinions differ on the constellation appropriate to the royal
Messiah. While it is generally agreed that the planet Jupiter indicated the advent of the Messiah, it is unclear to
which sign of the zodiac it was pointing as the Magi made
their journey.

At the time of Christ, Babylonian-Persian religion permeated Judaism and Hellenism. It would have been impossible to write the Gospels without using the thought-forms of pre-Christian religion, including the faith professed by the Magi, known today as 'cosmic religion.'[17]

The advent of the Magi in Jerusalem caused consternation in Herod's circle and beyond, and Matthew here allows us a rare insight into the cosmic dimension. The wise men belonged to a priestly caste that originated among the Medes and became the official priesthood of Zoroastrianism at a critical moment in the campaign of the Persian King Xerxes (*c.* 519–465 BC), according to the Greek historian Herodotus.[18] When 'the day was turned to night,' the Magi declared that the solar eclipse indicated Greek decline, and the moon Persian fortune.

When the stars returned to the same place in the heavens at the end of a Great Year, everything on earth began again in exactly the same way as before. According to the early Pythagorean, Hippasus, a Great Year comprised fifty-nine years in our reckoning.[19] So short a timespan is obviously not relative to all the planets but it is, as Waerden observes, a period in which Saturn and Jupiter return to nearly the same place in the sky, and therefore represents the interval which elapses between three conjunctions of Saturn and Jupiter (called Great Conjunctions).

The conjunction of Saturn and Jupiter

Discussion of the astronomical event of the Star of Bethlehem has returned again and again over the centuries to the triple conjunction of Saturn and Jupiter in the constellation of the Fishes in 7 BC. Interest in the Great Conjunction first surfaces in Christian literature in a long medieval poem ascribed to the Roman poet, Ovid:

> The astronomers say that every twenty years Jupiter
> meets his Father [Saturn] in conjunction ...[20]

In the thirteenth century, Roger Bacon *(c.* 1214–*c.* 1284)
adds to the picture:

> For me there is but one supreme influence, and that
> is the Blessed Virgin nursing her Son the Lord Jesus
> Christ, who is described by Albumazar [Abu Ma
> shar] in the sixth book of his Majus Introductorum,
> a description rendered still more vivid by the
> translation of Hermannus: 'In the first decan of
> Virgo there arises a girl, as the Persians, Chaldaeans,
> Egyptians and all writers from the earliest times
> relate: a pure virgin, a girl I say without blemish, or
> stain, of comely figure, charming features, modest in
> her bearing, having long hair, nursing a boy and
> feeding him broth in a place called Hebraea [land of
> the Hebrews], a boy I say, whom some people call
> Jesus and whom we call by the Greek name of
> Christ.'[21]

The author's meaning is that the figure of the Virgin is
depicted at the first ten degrees of Virgo, and that she was
born when the sun was in Virgo; and it is marked thus in
the calendar; and that she will nurse her son Jesus in the
land of the Hebrews.

KEPLER AND THE STAR OF BETHLEHEM

While there is a Great Conjunction (of Jupiter and Saturn)
every twenty years, the meeting point of the two planets
moves slowly around the zodiac, taking almost eight hun-

dred years to reappear in the same place. This cycle was known in ancient times:

> The Jewish astrologer called Mashallah (Messehalla in the West) was closely connected with the Persian tradition. He, like Abu Ma shar, came from Balkh, the city associated with Zoroaster. Abu Ma shar's book on conjunctions is concerned with the calculation of Saturn-Jupiter conjunctions and their astrological significance.[22]

These astrologers looked at the great period of eight hundred years and connected them with important events, such as the Deluge, the birth of Christ, the religion of Islam, and so on. A few centuries later, Tycho Brahe and Johannes Kepler's classic presentation of the Christian version of this doctrine is outlined in *De Stella Nova,* in volume I of Kepler's collected works.

Kepler recognized the 7 BC conjunction as introducing a new period of eight hundred years. At these intervals a major new religious figure is awaited. It is generally but wrongly supposed that the celebrated astronomer identified the conjunction as the Star of Bethlehem.[23]

In fact, Kepler believed that the star of Bethlehem was a Nova, a new star he supposed to have appeared at the time of the conjunction of Saturn, Jupiter and Mars in March 6 BC. He further believed that the Nativity followed in December, 5 BC, and the death of Herod in 4 BC.

The myth of Saturn and Jupiter

To realize the significance of the Saturn-Jupiter conjunction in ancient thought, we need to examine the mytholog-
ical and cosmic importance of these two celestial figures.
In antiquity Saturn and Jupiter represented the divine
Father and Son.[24]

There is yet another element in the picture, however, one
which illumines with even greater clarity the reason why
this planetary phenomenon is so significant. Yahweh, the
God of Israel, from an early period was identified with El,
the high father-god of Canaan and Phoenicia. We know
from Sanchuniathon, the priest of Beirut who left an extremely valuable account of Canaanite religion, that El was
the god of the planet Saturn, the 'Kronos' of the Greeks. In
Greek religion, of course, Kronos was dethroned by his son
Zeus, manifest in the planet Jupiter. This is paralleled in
Canaanite religion by the story of the rivalry between El
and Baal. Nonetheless, in Greek thought it is Kronos who
gives to Zeus 'all the measures of the whole creation,' because it is he who is 'the originator of times.' Here the conjunction of Saturn and Jupiter signified the transfer of
power from one planetary daemon to another. For the
Greeks and Phoenicians, El (Kronos) gave all his powers to
his son Baal (Zeus).

In Jewish theology El or Yahweh was still the universal
ruler, and the transfer of powers symbolized by the peri-
odic planetary conjunction meant something a bit different: Yahweh was giving his Messiah a portion of his
power and authority, so that he, the Messiah, might shat-
ter the wicked principalities that hold sway over the earth,
condemn them to punishment and exalt the righteous in
their stead. The planet Saturn in this cosmic drama repre-

sents Yahweh, while the planet Jupiter, called [in Hebrew] Sedeq [righteousness], represents his 'son,' the Messiah.

In the Gospel of Matthew we are left in no doubt that the overt reason for the Magi's visit was to show reverence at the birth of the royal Messiah. 'Where is the new-born king of the Jews?' is the only question they ask publicly. 'We have seen his star' informs Jerusalem that the Magi have been observing the planet Jupiter.

The Magi, it may be imagined, when they arrived in Jerusalem, would have explained to the chief priests and the scribes the significance of the recent triple conjunction of Saturn and Jupiter in 7 BC. It was incumbent upon them to explain to the Jewish theologians the Messianic significance of this phenomenon. Saturn was the star-sign of Old Testament religion,[25] and Jupiter would have been recognized as the planet of the Messiah. They would have given their interpretation of the Great Conjunction, signifying a transition from the Father (Yahweh) religion to the 'Son' religion of the Messiah.

After the Magi had adopted Zoroastrianism, they played an important part in the formation of the Cosmic Religion, with Plato as High Priest, which spread throughout the ancient world. Three centuries before the birth of Christ, the early Platonists were responsible for the development of a geometrical vision of the cosmos. In particular Heraclides Ponticus described the descent and ascent of the soul through seven planetary spheres. The soul descends to earth through the planetary gates which featured significantly in the rituals of Mithraism.

With their belief in spiritual events manifesting in cosmic happenings, a great soul entering incarnation would have appeared to the spiritual eye of the Magi as a radiant star. The Magi, then, contemplating the 7 BC conjunction of Saturn and Jupiter, may have concluded that at this time a significant soul, whom they may have connected with Zoroaster — the 'Golden Star' — entered the outer Saturn sphere, beginning descent to earth through the planetary gates.

Dating the arrival of the Magi

There is another element in the constellations which may help us date the arrival of the Magi more precisely. While Jupiter is the planet of the Messiah, the star sign Leo is the constellation of the royal Messiah.[26] Jupiter passes through the sign of Leo every twelve years, and would therefore have passed through Leo four or five years later than 7 BC when it was in Pisces. Jupiter entered the sidereal sign of Leo on September 18, 3 BC. About November 29, 3 BC, the planet came to rest and then began its retrograde motion (seen from the earth all planets move backwards, or retrograde, for a time, describing a loop). After looping Regulus, the king star of Leo, Jupiter re-entered Leo on May 16, 2 BC. In Babylon, looping Regulus signified a change of ruler in the East: the Parthian king Phraates IV duly died in 2 BC.

During the seven months that followed, Jupiter moved forward through the sign of Leo and into Virgo. It entered the sign of Virgo on October 17, 2 BC, coming to rest between December 24, 2 BC and January 3, 1 BC. We would therefore date the arrival of the Magi in Jerusalem during this period. Note that we have already dated the Nativity of Matthew's gospel to 6 January, 1 BC.

The story of the Magi following the star from the East loses nothing of its magical quality through an attempt to

*In those days a decree went out from Caesar Augustus
that all the world should be enrolled. This was the
first enrolment, when Quirinius was governor of Syria.
And all went to be enrolled, each to his own city. And
Joseph also went up from Galilee, from the city of
Nazareth, to Judea, to the city of David, which is
called Bethlehem, because he was of the house and
lineage of David, to be enrolled with Mary, his be-
trothed, who was with child. And while they were
there, the time came for her to be delivered. And she
gave birth to her first-born son and wrapped him in
swaddling cloths, and laid him in a manger, because
there was no place for them in the inn.*

*And in that region there were shepherds out in the
fields, keeping watch over their flock by night. And an
angel of the Lord appeared to them, and the glory of
the Lord shone around them, and they were filled with
fear. And the angel said to them, 'Be not afraid; for
behold, I bring you good news of great joy which will
come to all the people; for to you is born this day in
the city of David a Saviour, who is Christ the Lord.
And this will be a sign for you: you will find the
babe wrapped in swaddling clothes and lying in a
manger.' ...*

*And at the end of eight days, when he was circum-
cised, he was called Jesus, the name given by the
angel before he was conceived in the womb.*

*And when the time came for their purification
[after forty days] according to the law of Moses, they
brought him up to Jerusalem to present him to the
Lord.*

(Luke 2:1–12, 21f).

4. Luke's Nativity and the Enrolment

In his Gospel, Luke devotes much attention to the birth of both John the Baptist and Jesus, narrating the circumstances of the annunciation and birth at some length. Luke dates the annunciation of John's birth 'in the days of Herod, king of Judea' (1:5). Yet when we read of John's birth itself we can feel that the atmosphere has changed from the charged mood of Herod's last days in the Matthean birth story. At the end of Herod's life, the air was heavy with the fear of widespread bloodshed.[1]

The very different emotional spectrum of Luke's telling of events should also be noted. His story is abundant with awe, doubt, astonishment, humility, exaltation, tribulation, rejoicing and wonder, and excitement greets John's birth as the news sweeps through the land. Luke's narrative holds no mention of Herod's insane urge to slaughter and of the fear it engendered. Here, the lack of any official reaction stands in total contrast to the threatening violence and urgent flight of Matthew's account. Freedom from this fear can have only one explanation: the tyrant is dead.

It will be shown (see below, p.74) that a birth occurring at the time of the enrolment can only have taken place after Herod's death (January 28, 1 BC). Luke's indication, then, 'in the days of Herod the king' applies to the time of John's conception but not to the subsequent births of John and of Jesus of Nazareth. The only conclusion we can draw is that John and Jesus, according to Luke's account, were born in the period following Herod's death.

John the Baptist

> *In the days of Herod, king of Judea, there was a priest named Zechariah, of the division of Abijah; and he had a wife of the daughters of Aaron, and her name was Elizabeth. ... But they had no child, because Elizabeth was barren, and both were advanced in years.*
>
> *Now while he was serving as priest before God when his division was on duty, according to the custom of the priesthood, it fell on him to enter the temple of the Lord and burn incense. And the whole multitude of the people were praying outside at the house of incense. And there appeared to him an angel of the Lord ... the angel said to him, 'Do not be afraid, Zechariah, for your prayer is heard, and your wife Elizabeth will bear you a son, and you shall call his name John.'*
>
> (Luke 1:5, 7–9, 11–13).

We shall first examine a little more closely the timing of the annunciation of John the Baptist's birth. Luke (1:5,8) states that, at that time, John's father Zechariah was serving his turn of duty in the Temple belonging, as he did, to the priests' course of Abijah. Chronological interpretation of this statement is problematic. According to the First Book of the Chronicles (24:7–19) the first course to serve in the rota was Jehoiarib, which was appointed to serve for a week commencing on the Sabbath, before being relieved by the next course. The course of Abijah, to which Zechariah belonged, was the eighth of twenty-four courses. Unfortunately we are not told the time of year when each course served.

We do know, however, that the first course of Jehoiarib was serving on Ab 9, August 6, AD 70 when the Temple was

Jewish date	Julian date	Course
Ab 8-14	August 5-11	1 Jehoiarib
Ab 15-21	August 12-18	2 Jedaiah
Ab 22-28	August 19-25	3 Harim
Ab 29-Elul 6	August 26-Sep 1	4 Seorim
Elul 7-13	September 2-8	5 Malchijah
Elul 14-20	September 9-15	6 Mijamin
Elul 21-27	September 16-22	7 Hakkoz
Elul 28-Tishri 4	September 23-29	8 Abijah

Table 3. Priests' courses due to serve in AD 70.

destroyed by the Romans. Both Talmuds, the *Tosefta* (a collection only less ancient than the Mishnah) and in the *Chronicle Seder Olam Tabbah,* Rabbi Jose ben Halafta (c. AD 150) report on this point.[2] Had the Temple not been destroyed in AD 70, they would have continued to serve as shown in Table 3.

Each course served one week twice a year, apart from the joint participation of all courses at the time of the three pilgrim festivals. Table 3 shows that Abijah was due to serve at the New Year in the autumn of AD 70. Assuming that the pattern was repeated each year Zechariah also would have served at autumn New Year in 2 BC. This corresponds to a birth at the traditional midsummer.

Luke informs us that a large number of people were present while Zechariah was making the offering, 'the whole number of people' presumably implying that the day was of more than ordinary importance.[3] Table 3 identifies the special day as the autumn New Year's day Tishri 1, October 1, 2 BC. John's birth would then follow nine months later, around Ab 9, June 30, 1 BC.

The enrolment

This much-discussed passage presents great difficulties to
the historian. Five issues have been identified:

1. History does not otherwise record a general imperial
   census in the time of Augustus.
2. Under a Roman census, Joseph would not have been
   obliged to travel to Bethlehem, and Mary would not
   have been required to accompany him there.
3. A Roman census could not have been carried out in
   Palestine during the time of King Herod.
4. Josephus knows nothing of a Roman census in Palestine
   during the reign of Herod; he refers rather to the census
   of AD 6–7 as something new and unprecedented.
5. A census held under Quirinius could not have taken
   place in the time of Herod, for Quirinius was never governor of Syria during Herod's lifetime.[4]

Luke makes additional mention of the census in Acts 5:37:

> After him Judas the Galilean arose in the days of the
> census [*apographe* in Greek] and drew away some
> of the people after him; he also perished, and all
> who followed him were scattered.

Since the Gospel account is much more complex, we
shall begin with the reference in Acts. It is most interesting
that in Luke's report of Gamaliel's speech, the enrolment is
connected with the origin of the Zealot movement headed
by Judas the Galilean. Since Josephus attributed the destruction of Jerusalem by the Romans in AD 70 to the un-
bridled fanaticism of these Zealot movements, we are able

to trace their origins in his history. If we can date the beginning of the Zealot movement, it would help to establish the timing of the census.

In Josephus also, the taxation under Quirinius in AD 6–7 is linked to the rebellion of Judas.

> Quirinius, a Roman senator ... arrived in Syria, dispatched by Caesar to be governor [or judge] of the nation and to make an assessment of their property ... Quirinius also visited Judea, which had been annexed to Syria, in order to make an assessment of the property of the Jews and to liquidate the estate of Archelaus. Although the Jews were at first shocked to hear of the registration [*apographe*] of property, they gradually condescended, yielding to the arguments of the High Priest Joazar, the son of Boethus, to go no further in opposition. So those who were convinced by him declared, without shilly-shallying, the value of their property. But a certain Judas, a Gaulanite, from a city named Gamala, who had enlisted the aid of Saddok, a Pharisee, threw himself into the cause of rebellion. They said that the assessment carried with it a status amounting to downright slavery ...[5]

Judas of Gamala has been identified with Judas son of Ezekias (Hezekiah), who already figured in *Antiquities*.[6] Ezekias, a dangerous adversary, had been unceremoniously executed by the young Herod.[7] His son Judas was prominent in the disturbances which followed Herod's death. Varus, Roman governor of Syria at the time of Herod's death, intervened when the rapacious Sabinus, the procurator of Caesar, set out to 'take charge' of Herod's property.

This was at least half the kingdom, it is estimated. Josephus
continues:

> Then there was Judas the son of the brigand-chief
> Ezekias, who had been a man of great power and
> had been captured by Herod only with great
> difficulty. This Judas got together a large number
> of desperate men at Sepphoris in Galilee and there
> made an assault on the royal palace, and having
> seized all the arms that were stored there, he armed
> every single one of his men and made off with all
> the property that had been seized there. He became
> an object of terror to all men by plundering those
> he came across in his desire for great possessions
> and his ambition for royal rank, a prize that he
> expected to obtain not through the practice of
> virtue but through excessive ill-treatment of
> others.[8]

Varus sent his son to fight against the Galileans, and
Sepphoris, the most important city in Galilee which was
the centre of the rebellion, was burnt to the ground and its
inhabitants sold into slavery. At the same time, Varus pro-
ceeded to Samaria where he encountered no opposition.[9]
On the single occasion when Augustus is recorded as inter-
vening in Palestinian fiscal affairs, in the determination of
Herod's testament Augustus rewarded Samaria for its loy-
alty with a tax remission.

> [Herod] Antipas [second surviving son of Herod the
> Great] received the revenue of Peraea and Galilee,
> which yielded an annual tribute of two hundred
> talents ... To Archelaus [first surviving son of Herod]

both Idumaea and Judea were made subject and also
the district of the Samaritans, who had a fourth of
their tribute remitted by Caesar; this alleviation he
decreed because they had not joined the rest of the
people in revolting.[10]

Archelaus had sent his steward to bring accounts of
Herod's property to Augustus.[11] Caesar Augustus is thus
seen involved in an assessment of Herod's kingdom, as required by Luke's narrative. Before the Roman annexation
of Judea in AD 6, the taxation system was controlled by the
Herods. As Schürer observes,[12] Herod acted independently
throughout with regard to tax and there is no sign whatever
of his paying any dues to the Romans. He remitted and
even exempted from taxation at will. Indeed one of the
complaints made to Augustus by the Jewish deputation before his adjudication of Herod's testament concerned 'the
collecting of the tribute that was imposed on everyone each
year,' for Herod's demands were excessive and his methods
irregular and arbitrary. On this occasion Augustus was suf-
ficiently involved that he did not rely on the accounts of
Archelaus' steward. It is distinctly stated that he received
revenue reports from Varus and Sabinus.

When Caesar had read these letters and also the
reports of Varus and Sabinus concerning the
amount of the property and the size of the annual
revenue, and had looked at the various letters sent
by Antipas in an effort to obtain the kingship for
himself, he called together his friends to give their
opinions. Among them he gave first place at his
side to Gaius ...[13]

At this time Gaius was about nineteen years old and favoured to succeed his grandfather Augustus. He was about to take up his proconsular appointment in Syria and it was obviously beneficial to his authority to be seen by his subjects appearing at the side of the Emperor. To raise the esteem of the inexperienced youth in the eyes of the soldiery, Gaius was married to the empress's grand-daughter Livilla presumably in Rome before his departure with a distinguished entourage. Among them was Publius Sulpicius Quirinius.

There is no doubt that Quirinius was the ideal man to clear up the disorder left by Varus. Quirinius combined administrative competence of a high order with a taste for the unpleasant business of the registration. When, a few years later, Archelaus was deposed, Quirinius was again charged with the task.

We may now consider whether:

1. The *apographe* is supposed to have been a Roman taxation conducted at some time during Herod's lifetime.
2. The *apographe* was a valuation of Herod's estate made in the months following his death in 1 BC.
3. Luke's *apographe* was the taxing of Judea in AD 6–7 by Quirinius, recorded by Josephus.

The first possibility seems to be excluded because:

> ... Josephus knows nothing of a Roman census in Palestine during the time of Herod. One is, admittedly, disinclined to place too much reliance on *argumenta e silentio*. But in this case it has meaning. On no other period is Josephus so well informed, on none is he so thorough, as on that of

Herod's last years. It is almost inconceivable that he would have ignored a measure such as a Roman census of that time, which would have offended people to the quick, whilst faithfully describing the census of AD 6/7, which occurred in a period of which he reports very much less. It should be borne in mind that a Roman census left behind it an effect; like that of AD 6/7 it would have provoked a revolt.[14]

It is therefore important that Luke's enrolment should not be identified with the taxation of Judea in AD 6–7 (which would not have affected the Galilean subjects of Herod Antipas) but rather with the assessment of Herod's estate following his death. Although supervised by the Romans, it was conducted along traditional Jewish lines according to tribes and genealogies. It was completed in the months after Varus had ceased to be governor of Syria in 1 BC. During this transitional period in early winter 1 BC, practical authority for administration was probably divided between Gaius' principal aides, Lollius and Quirinius. In the circumstances it is likely that Quirinius would have been given full authority to settle the affairs of Palestine in the winter of 1 BC.

F. Heichelheim dismisses the possibility that Luke was mistaken in placing the Nativity in the setting of an enrolment.[15] Writing in the first century only a generation or so after the life of Christ, Luke could and would have been refuted or corrected by both non-Christians and Christians living near Bethlehem and also by the family of Jesus living there. There was no Roman census before Quirinius, 'but it is generally forgotten that half or two-thirds of Herod's kingdom was his private domain, and that a census

must have been held [after his death] in these regions to fa-
cilitate the collection of poll and land taxes which were di-
rectly owed to the king.'

Luke, on the above analysis, need not be corrected on
any specific point if something like the following para-
phrase is deemed to be permissible:

> In the days following Herod's death, Caesar
> Augustus ordered that Herod's entire kingdom
> should be assessed for tax purposes. This was the
> earlier of two enrolments conducted while Quirinius
> was governor of Syria. And all went to be enrolled
> for the poll and property tax, each to his own
> ancestral city, in the Jewish manner. And Joseph also
> went up from Galilee, from a settlement called
> Nazareth, to Judea, to the city of David, which is
> called Bethlehem, because he was of the house and
> lineage of David, to be enrolled with Mary, his
> betrothed, who was with child.

The birth of Jesus

Luke places the annunciation of the birth of Jesus six
(lunar) months after that of John, that is on Nisan 1, March
26, 1 BC (Luke 1:26). The resultant date of the Nativity,
which in antiquity was reckoned to follow after a gestation
period of 10 sidereal months (273 days), is Tebeth 9,
December 25, 1 BC.

Again, the traditional dating of the Nativity came long
before its establishment as a fixed feast-day in the cycle of
the Christian year. Already Hippolytus (*c.* 170–*c.* 235) in
his *Commentary of Daniel,* dated the birth of Jesus eight
days before the Calends of January (December 25). But

Christmas, like many comparable festivals, was not celebrated on a certain day much before the middle of the
fourth century, when the Christian year came into being.
The earliest mention of the Feast of the Nativity on
December 25 is in Rome in AD 354. In this year an entry in
the *Depositio Martyrum* reads, *VIII Kal. Ianuarii natus
Christus in Betleem Iudaea.*'[16]

> *In the fifteenth year of the reign of Tiberius Caesar,*
> *Pontius Pilate being governor of Judea, and Herod*
> *being Tetrarch of Galilee and his brother Philip*
> *Tetrarch of the region of Ituraea and Trachonitis,*
> *and Lysanias Tetrarch of Abilene, in the high-*
> *priesthood of Annas and Caiaphas, the word of*
> *God came to John the son of Zechariah in the*
> *wilderness; and he went into all the region about*
> *the Jordan, preaching a baptism of repentance for*
> *the forgiveness of sins.*
>
> (Luke 3,1)

5. The Baptism of Jesus

The beginning of John the Baptist's ministry in the fifteenth year of Tiberius Caesar can be viewed against the
background of the Essenes' quest for spiritual perfection in
the remoteness of the desert. At the Essene centre of
Qumran, John was a familiar figure. Far from the cities, the
Essenes bestowed their baptism on the few who had
reached the requisite degree of perfection.

It is generally thought that John began his work in the
autumn season, when the intense summer heat was abating
and attention turned to the religious festivals of repentance
and atonement. At that time the faithful would have been
attending the solemn ceremonies in the Temple. It seems
that John's first audience in the desert was made up largely
of soldiers and tax-collectors (Luke 3:12), classes of people hardly known for their piety and for whom the devo-
tions of the Essenes would have been unapproachable.
What, then, were these religious untouchables doing down
by the Jordan when John began his ministry?

A historian's picture of the unhospitable nature of the
scene only underlines the question:

> The surrounding view was sheer desolation. At
> John's feet twisted and turned the Jordan in its
> narrow, deep-sunk trough. No longer was its water
> bright, clear green as when it left the Lake of
> Galilee; its rapid flow deeper and deeper into the

earth, to which it owed its name 'Descender,' had charged its waters with mud to the point of saturation. ...

To either side, valley and sea were shut in by lines of unscalable hills, broken rarely by gorges through which trails climbed up by the plateau. The rocks were almost unbelievably barren, thrown about in wild confusion ... In winter, wind passed over snow-covered Hermon at the valley head and whistled down the narrow trough; in summer the hills shut in an intolerable heat the few unfortunate peasants who tended Jericho's balsam wealth for absentee landlords. To the heat and the ever-present malaria was added the unrealized but not unfelt atmospheric pressure, which makes mere breathing a misery, for the spot is actually the lowest open to the sun on earth, almost thirteen hundred feet below the level of the sea.[1]

The rite of baptism

John could not have begun his preaching without a congregation, and the gathering of people he found by the Jordan was presumably assembling for another purpose. But for what purpose? A theologian provides an answer which is partially satisfying.

The weeks preceding the Day of Atonement were always a time of preparation for that great fast, and the Jewish motif of that season was *teshubah'* (repentance) and *Malkut Shamayim'* (the Kingdom of Heaven) ... The baptism of John thus heralded the approach of the establishment of the New Covenant

founded on forgiveness of sins (Jer.31:31–34), as
the Old Covenant on Sinai was preceded by
'sanctification' (Exod.19:10), which in the earliest
Midrash is actually called 'baptism' [compare my
edition of Sifre, 92]. One of the prophetic lessons
for this season was the latter portion of Micah 7; cf.
v.19, 'and thou wilt cast all their sins into the depths
of the sea.' (This verse has given rise at a later date
to a quaint Jewish custom retained until this day. On
one of the days between New Year and the Day of
Atonement the people go down to any neighbouring
sheet of water and shake their garments into it,
thereby symbolically disposing of their sins. This
little drama is called *Tashlich* — 'thou wilt cast').
As straws are capable of indicating the quarter from
which the wind blows, so these small matters
suggest the probability that John began his ministry
about this season ...[2]

Theodor Gaster provides a historical perspective on the
origins of *Tashlich:*

In the afternoon of the first day of New Year (or of
the second day, if the first happens on a Sabbath), it
is the practice of orthodox Jews to repair to the
nearest body of flowing water and there recite in
Hebrew the closing words of the biblical book of
Micah ...
The custom is first attested in the fifteenth
century, and it is explained in a purely homiletic
manner. According to one's view, the sight of the
water on New Year's Day is intended to recall the
fact that the world was created out of watery chaos;

while another insists that the purpose of visiting
flowing streams is to observe the fish and thereby to
be reminded that, in the word of the Preacher,
mankind is 'as the fishes that are caught in an evil
net' (Eccles.9:12). Yet a third interpretation sees in
the custom an allusion to the ancient legend which
relates that when Abraham was speeding to Mount
Moriah in obedience to the divine commandment to
sacrifice his son Isaac —an event which was said to
have taken place on New Year's Day — Satan
interposed a turbid stream to impede his progress.
The patriarch, however, would not be stayed, but
strode through it undaunted!

The true origin of the ceremony is probably to be
found, however, in the common custom of throwing
sops to the spirits of rivers on critical days of the
year. The Romans, for example, used to cast straw
puppets into the Tiber at the Ides of May; in
European folk-usage, such offerings are (or were)
often made to Rhine, Danube, Rhone, Elbe and
Neckar on New Year's Eve. The Jews would thus
have adopted the custom from their Gentile
neighbours, reinterpreting it in accordance with their
own outlook and tradition.[3]

The emergence of John the Baptist

The beginning of John's Baptism can thus be associated
with *Tashlich,* which can be traced to an earlier pagan rite
practised on the New Year's Eve in the autumn early in our
era.[4] Like the Jewish New Year, the pagan or civil New Year
also had its rite of repentance. The tax collectors, soldiers
and the multitudes had probably adopted the method of sal-

vation of surrounding Gentile cults. The words of the Baptist lend themselves to this reading. 'You brood of vipers' is a particularly vituperative way of referring to the Serpent spirit which played such a role in pagan rites. And upon these offspring of the Serpent, John conferred the sacred baptism of the exclusive Essenes. No more dramatic emergence could be imagined.

We date John's emergence then to the civil New Year's eve, Heshvan 1, October 8, AD 28. L. Girard confirms that the fifteenth year of Tiberius is equivalent to AD 28–29, saying that it is certain that the Latin authors Tacitus, Suetonius, Pliny, the Christian chronologists Julian Africanus, Hippolytus, Tertullian, Lanctantius, Eusebius, the Jewish historian Josephus ... in a word the whole of antiquity, pagan, Jewish and Christian have known but one chronology of Tiberius in which AD 14–15 is always the starting point from which the fifteenth year of Tiberius is always reckoned as AD 28–29.[5]

The Baptism of Jesus

John's baptism of Jesus is dated according to second-century tradition on January 6. It has been reasonably conjectured that the date must have derived from a tradition concerning the length of the Christ's ministry. Such sometimes inconsistent traditions are to be found set down side by side, for instance, in Dionysius Exiguus (*c.* 500– *c.* 560). Dionysius writes, '... and from when he was baptized Jesus Christ our Lord were two years and 90 days, which are 820 days ...'

Counting that number of days forward from January 6 yields a date of April 5, easily recognizable as April 5, AD 33, the date of the Resurrection. Counting back two years and ninety days earlier (820 days) from the Resurrection, the Baptism of Jesus is accordingly dated January 6, AD 31. Counting back again from that date in AD 31, it is of interest to note that the very same interval of 820 days brings us to our date for the beginning of John's ministry (October 8, AD 28).

After the Baptism

The chronological problem further explored below is to connect possible models of the Incarnation with the data in the Gospels, and with extant traditions concerning the duration of the ministry. On the latter point Dionysius Exiguus (*c.* 550–*c.* 560) collected disparate strands of wildly conflicting traditions:

> From March 25 to December 25 the days number 271. From the resultant number of days Christ our Lord was conceived on the day of the Lord (Sunday) March 25 and born on Tuesday December 25. On the day of his Passion 133 (*sic!*) years and 3 months had passed, which is 12,414 days. Again it is stated that he was born on Tuesday December 25 and died on Friday March 25. Counting from the Baptism were two years and 90 days, or 820 days from the day on which he was baptized Thursday, January 6, and suffered on Friday March 25, as already stated.[6]

Among the examples provided by Dionysius, the ministry is stated as beginning on January 6 and ending on March 25 after an interval of 820 days. But 820 days from January 6 brings us to April 5, not March 25. The nearest approximation to the figures is achieved by dating the Baptism Saturday January 6, AD 31 and — after 820 days — the Resurrection on Sunday April 5, AD 33. There is no tradition of the year of the Baptism and it is supposed that the date January 6 was deduced from a tradition relating to the length of the ministry.

As cited in Chapter 3, the earliest tradition of the date January 6 is found in Clement of Alexandria *(c.* 150– *c.* 215):

> And the followers of Basilides [Gnostics of a Petrine school] hold the day of his baptism as a festival, spending the night before in readings. And they say that it was in the fifteenth year of Tiberius Caesar, the fifteenth day of the month Tubi; and some say that it was the eleventh of the same month, [that is, January 6 or 10].[7]

Never explicitly stated in antiquity, there seem to have been two traditions which hover over many statements of early Christian writers. Firstly the Baptism was linked with the date of the Nativity in the Eastern tradition of January 6. Secondly, the Crucifixion is connected with the day of the Annunciation, March 25, according to Western tradition.

> *Jesus, when he began his ministry, was about thirty years of age.*
>
> (Luke 3:23)

6. The Crucifixion

It is wholly appropriate that the Crucifixion, the culminating outcome of the life of Jesus, should also be the most important event in dating his birth historically. In the main two possibilities for the year of the Crucifixion are favoured by modern biblical chronologists: AD 30 and AD 33. Following normal practice, the result obtained depends on the interpretation placed upon the fifteenth year of Tiberius and the estimated length of Jesus' ministry.

The fifteenth year of Tiberius

Many scholars have thought the date Tiberius 15 so important that Luke (3:1) must have meant it applied to the baptism of Jesus, not merely to the opening of John's ministry. It is generally agreed that the fifteenth year of Tiberius was AD 28–29. However, we must again distinguish carefully between the civil and ecclesiastical calendars in Palestine (see Chapter 1).

The identification of Tiberius 15 in the civil calendar with autumn AD 28–29 is confirmed by a coin of Q. Caecilius Silanus, governor of Syria AD 12–17. The coin is numbered 45 (of the Actian era) and bears the head of Tiberius, dated with the letter A (equivalent to Tiberius 1). Since the beginning of the Actian era is dated autumn 31 BC in Syria, Actian 45 is equivalent to Tiberius 1 which began in autumn AD 14, and Tiberius 15 began in autumn AD 28 (see Appendix).

The year in the ecclesiastical calendar corresponding to autumn AD 28–29 is spring AD 29–30. This conclusion is strengthened by the connection between the beginning of John's ministry and the pagan (autumn) New Year ceremony discussed above (p. 84). If we equate (civil) autumn AD 28–29 with (ecclesiastical) spring AD 29–30, this means that the earliest possible Passover of Jesus' ministry is spring AD 29.

The length of Jesus' ministry

John mentions three Passovers in the course of Jesus' ministry.[1] According to the above calculation, the earliest these could have fallen was in spring AD 29, 30 and 31. Unless we are to limit Jesus' ministry to a single year, AD 29–30, this makes it impossible to conclude that the Crucifixion took place as early as AD 30.

Following the time indications in the Gospels themselves, we can trace a period of about twenty-seven months as the duration of Jesus' ministry. This falls into three separate periods of around nine months: the so-called silent ministry, the teaching ministry, and the period of the Transfiguration.

THE SILENT MINISTRY

We can allocate a period of about eight or nine months to what Stauffer has called Jesus' 'silent ministry,' a period following the Baptism in the Jordan, and before he began his public teaching ministry in Galilee. Table 4 (page 97) suggests a likely chronology for this period and its principal events. It is the Gospel of John which, in its first five chapters, chiefly describes this ministry, with its two journeys into Galilee.

This period includes Jesus' temptation in the wilderness, the calling of the disciples, the marriage at Cana, and the cleansing of the Temple. Its end is marked by the arrest of John the Baptist.

According to Stauffer,[2] Jesus evidently first learned of the arrest of John at the feast of the Jews (John 5:1), namely Tabernacles. Stauffer envisages that Herod Antipas was embarked on a pilgrimage to celebrate the Day of Atonement and the ensuing Feast of Tabernacles in Jerusalem when he sought out John. In that case John would have been arrested immediately before the Day of Atonement which in AD 31 was on Sunday, Tishri 10, (September 16).

THE TEACHING MINISTRY

Around the moment of John's arrest, Jesus makes a third journey from Judea to Galilee, a journey marking the start of his public ministry.

Now after John was arrested, Jesus came into Galilee, preaching the gospel of God and saying, 'The time is fulfilled and the kingdom of God is at hand; repent and believe in the gospel.' (Mark 1:14f. See also Luke 4:14–16)

The continuation of the story of Jesus' ministry now moves from John's Gospel to Luke:

And he came to Nazareth, where he had been brought up; and he went to the synagogue, as his custom was, on the sabbath day. And he stood up to read; and there was given to him the book [scroll] of

the prophet Isaiah. He opened the book and found
the place where it was written,

'The Spirit of the Lord is upon me,
because he has anointed me to preach good news
   to the poor.
He has sent me to proclaim release to the captives
and recovering of sight to the blind,
to set at liberty those who are oppressed,
to proclaim the acceptable year of the Lord.'

And he closed the book, and gave it back to the
attendant, and sat down; and the eyes of all in the
synagogue were fixed on him. And he began to say
to them, 'Today this scripture has been fulfilled in
your hearing.' (Luke 4:17–21)

Questions arise out of this passage. Can this Sabbath be
dated? Is the reading from Isaiah specially selected by the
Christ or, if not, can it be placed in the Jewish reading
cycle? These questions begin to find their answer in a
closer knowledge of the Jewish synagogue service for the
Sabbath.

The service of the synagogue was not unlike our
own. After the prayers two lessons were always
read, one from the Law called *parashah,* and one
from the Prophets called *haphtarah;* and as there
were no ordained ministers to conduct the
services ... these lessons might not only be read
by any competent person who received per-
mission from the *rôsh hak-kenéseth,* but he was
even at liberty to add his own *midrash,* or
comment.[3]

A respected Jewish scholar, J. Mann finds 'ample evidence' that at the time of Christ, this text from Isaiah 61:1f formed part of the lectionary cycle, as indicated in Luke 4.[4] Other scholars also invoke the lectionary evidence when dating the start of the Galilean ministry: 'It seems likely, therefore, that our Lord's synagogue sermon was preached shortly afterwards, at the end of Tishri or the beginning of Cheshvan [Heshvan].'[5]

Basing ourselves on this evidence, we would also date the beginning of the Galilean teaching ministry from the Sabbath of the synagogue sermon (Luke 4:14ff). Coming soon after Tabernacles (September 21-28, AD 31), the Sabbath in question can be dated to Tishri 30 (October 6) AD 31.

THE TRANSFIGURATION

The ministry of the Lord reached a high point in the event of the Transfiguration, when Jesus took three disciples up a mountain and was transfigured before them (Luke 9:28–36). There are two traditional dates: Tammuz 17 (June/July) and, in the modern calendar, August 6, and we can hazard a guess at the tradition which is expressed in these divergent dates. Translated into the historical year in question, these commemorative dates correspond to Tammuz 17, July 14, and Ab 9, August 6, AD 32.

Both dates are connected with the fall of Jerusalem. In the Mishnah both the first fall of Jerusalem in 587 BC and the second fall in AD 70 are commemorated on 17 Tammuz. It seems probable that the burning of the Temple was seen by early Christians as an image of the Transfiguration. For the Temple was destroyed on Ab 9, August 6, in AD 70. And in the year of the Transfiguration AD 32, Ab 9 is (as in

AD 70) August 6. The conflagration which engulfed the Temple of Jerusalem in AD 70 must indeed have been an awe-inspiring spectacle.

Faced with a choice for the date of the Transfiguration between the Julian equivalents of Tammuz 17 and Ab 9, the Church of Jerusalem seems to have chosen Tammuz 17, July 14, while the Greek Church preferred Ab 9, August 6. Based on the cycle of Gospel readings through the year, we favour the date of the Transfiguration as Tammuz 17, July 14.[6]

The main events and probable length of the ministry of Christ can now be summarized as a whole, showing the periods relating to the three Passovers, in Table 4 (page 97).

Pontius Pilate

The Crucifixion is attested everywhere to have been carried out under Pontius Pilate as procurator of Judea. His dispatch as successor to Valerius Gratus is recorded by Josephus who dates his appointment as AD 26.[7] His recall is mentioned with the date of his dismissal as AD 36: 'And so Pilate, after having spent ten years in Judea, hurried to Rome in obedience to the orders of Vitellius, since he could not refuse.'[8] Apart from the references in Josephus, there are coins of the procurator dated Tiberius 16, Tiberius 17 and Tiberius 18, that is, AD 29–32.[9] Pilate's term of office was therefore AD 26 to AD 36.

Do the Trial scenes in the Gospels fit better into the earlier (AD 30) or later (AD 33) period of Pilate's rule? In the Gospels, the governor appears in a not unsympathetic light, weak and vacillating but inclined to be just. By contrast, a nearly contemporary pen portrait, written in AD 40, has him provocatively anti-Semitic, naturally inflexible, a blend of

Year	Jewish date	Julian date	Weekday	
AD 31	Tebeth 23	January 6	Saturday	Baptism of Jesus
	c. Adar 2	*c.* February 15	(Thursday)	Temptation
	c. Adar 4-8	*c.* Feb 16-20	(Fri-Tue)	Calling of the disciples
	Adar 16	February 27	Tuesday	Marriage at Cana
	Nisan 10	March 23	Friday	Cleansing of the Temple
	Sivan 9	May 20	Sunday	Samaritan Pentecost
	c. Tishri 7-8	*c.* Sept 13-14	(Thu-Fri)	Arrest of John
	Tishri 16	September 22	Saturday	Healing of paralytic
	Tishri 30	October 6	Saturday	Opening of the Galilean ministry
AD 32	Nisan 1	April 1	Tuesday	Death of John
	c. Nisan 16-20	*c.* April 16-20	(Wed-Sat)	Feeding of five thousand
	c. Sivan 6-11	*c.* June 2-8	(Mon-Sat)	Feeding of four thousand
	Tammuz 9	July 6	Sunday	Confession of Peter
	Tammuz 17	July 14	Monday	Transfiguration
	Tishri 15-22	October 10-17	Fri-Fri	Tabernacles in Jerusalem
	Kislev 25	December 18	Thursday	Feast of Dedication
AD 33	Tebeth 15	January 6	Tuesday	At the Jordan (John 10:40)
	c. Adar 4-8	*c.* February 23	(Monday)	Raising of Lazarus
	Nisan 1	March 21	Saturday	New Jubilee cycle

Table 4. The events of the three years of Christ's ministry.

self-will and relentlessness.[10] Why, when we read the Gospels, are we not given the picture of a mass-murderer, arbitrary and scornful of due process of law?

It has been suggested that Pilate was a creature of Tiberius' effective ruler, Sejanus. Exercising almost unlimited power in Rome, Sejanus was characterized by a strong anti-Semitism not shared by Tiberius. After the disgrace and death of Sejanus on October 18, AD 31, Tiberius took the government into his own hands again. Before autumn 31, Pilate was secure in Sejanus' favour, and even flagrant anti-Semitism in Jerusalem would have been applauded in Rome. After the death of Sejanus, Tiberius frowned upon signs of Pilate's misrule, as his ultimate recall shows.[11] This analysis is compatible with the Trial falling in the year 33 but not with the year 30.

The eclipse of the moon

Events can be dated with precision only when the timing can be fixed through the use of astronomical data. Thus great attention should be paid to the two lunar eclipses which occurred around the time of the birth and death of Jesus. There was an eclipse shortly before Herod's death, to which reference has already been made, which therefore plays an important role in the chronology of the Nativity. The second eclipse of the moon occurred on April 3, AD 33.

The latter eclipse had not been recognized as significant in chronological discussion until C.J. Humphreys and W.G. Waddington published their article in *Nature* in 1983. These two Oxford scientists quote a number of examples from the ancient world in which 'the moon turning to blood' was used as the technical term for a lunar eclipse. A quotation from the Old Testament prophet Joel in Peter's first Pentecost sermon (Acts 2:14–20) provides their starting point:

> But Peter, standing with the eleven, lifted up his voice and addressed them, 'Men of Judea and all who dwell in Jerusalem, let this be known to you, and give ear to my words. For these men are not drunk, as you suppose, since it is only the third hour of the day; but this is what was spoken by the prophet Joel:
>
> '"And in the last days it shall be, God declares, that I will pour out my Spirit upon all flesh, and your sons and your daughters shall prophesy, and your young men shall see visions, and your old men shall dream dreams; yea, and on my menservants and my maidservants in those days I will pour out my Spirit; and they shall prophesy. And I will show wonders in the heaven above and signs on the earth beneath, blood, and fire, and vapour of smoke; The sun will be turned into darkness and the moon into blood, before the day of the Lord comes, the great and manifest day".'

Humphreys and Waddington write:

> The quotation from Joel provides a telling commentary on the recent events of the first Easter. The outpouring of Spirit commenced at Pentecost and 'that great and glorious day' refers to the resurrection. 'The sun will be turned to darkness' (Acts 2:20) is a clear reference to the three hours of darkness at the crucifixion (Matt.27:45), and would be

understood as such by Peter's audience. Since the
darkened sun occurred at the crucifixion, it is
reasonable to suppose that 'the moon turned to
blood' that same evening.[12]

It seems unlikely, the authors say, that Peter should
proclaim as the first words uttered with the inspiration of
the Whitsuntide Spirit an Old Testament quotation without particular application to events less than two months
old.

Humphreys and Waddington believe that Peter's Joel
quotation at Pentecost refers to the darkness at noon on the
day of the crucifixion and, on the same day, an eclipse of
the moon. The article shows the moon 'turning to blood' to
be in ancient times a not unusual description of a lunar
eclipse. The following examples are cited:

1. The lunar eclipse of September 20, 331 BC occurred two
   days after Alexander crossed the Tigris, and the moon
   was described by Curtius as 'suffused with the colour of
   blood.'[13]
2. The lunar eclipse of August 31, AD 304 (probably) which
   occurred at the martyrdom of Bishop Felix, was described in *Acta Sanctorum* as 'when he was about to be
   martyred the moon was turned to blood.'
3. The lunar eclipse of March 2, AD 462, was described in
   the *Hydatius Lemicus Chronicon* thus: 'on March 2
   with the crowing of cocks after the setting of the sun the
   full moon was turned to blood.'

This forms the basis of the argument that at Pentecost
Peter quoted Joel (2:31) in connection with an eclipse of
the Passover moon at the Crucifixion. F. R. Stephenson

already identified this quotation as referring to a lunar eclipse.[14]

We find in the Book of Revelation (6:12) a prophecy which closely resembles Joel's: 'there was a great earthquake; and the sun became black as sackcloth, the full moon became like blood.' The point of interest in this quotation is that it is the full moon that becomes like blood. Astronomically, only the full moon can be eclipsed, just as only a new moon can eclipse the sun. The apocalyptist by mentioning the full moon reveals that he does not attribute the darkening of the sun to a solar eclipse. And by the same token the blood-red full moon most likely indicates that he has a lunar eclipse in mind. Yet if Peter's hearers understood his words in this way, is it not puzzling that this interpretation is not found much more prominently stated in early Christian literature?

Regarding the darkening of the sun at the Crucifixion, Luke and his contemporaries were perfectly aware that a solar eclipse at the full moon was an astronomical impossibility. The verb *eklejpein,* 'to fail,' while a technical term for an eclipse, is also used to describe the sun's (or moon's) light failing for whatever reason. It has been suggested that the darkness at noon was caused by a *khamsin* storm which is not unexpected during the fifty days between Easter and Pentecost. The *khamsin,* an Arabic word meaning 'fifty,' is an extremely dry, hot and dust-laden wind which blows up from the desert. Also called 'simoom,' the dust-storm causes a darkening which at its most intense can be compared to the effect of a total solar eclipse.

> The cunning yellow devil of the *khamsin* is worse than the black storm devil. Clouds of dust swirl skyward out of the Arabian desert while the air at

ground level scarcely stirs. It is felt only in the
mouth filled with grit, in the effort of breathing, the
reddened eyes ... Over sky and earth, like smoke
from a fire, swirl dirty yellow clouds, and the red
sun peers bleakly through like a bloody sphere.
Suddenly, the coolness of the night is replaced by
oppressive heat that feels as if it were streaming out
of a glowing oven. An odour of sulphur, asphalt and
tar seeps across from the Dead Sea ... Grass and
flowers in the fields droop. Birdsong ceases. Sheep
bleat and cows moo woefully. Dogs wander around
with hanging tongues; people are gripped by a
feeling that is like a presentiment of impending,
inescapable disaster. It is as if the threatening
shadow of primal chaos and the coming world's end
were moving across earth and heaven.[15]

During the Crucifixion, the sun was blotted out. Since
the darkness lasted only three hours, there must have been
a fresh wind clearing the thick atmosphere at the time of
the earthquake which rent the veil of the Temple at about
3.00 pm, the hour of Christ's death (Matt.27:51).

These, in outline, are the grounds for accepting that at
Pentecost Peter quoted Joel in conjunction with the eclipse
of the Passover moon at the Crucifixion. For the first time
positive evidence has been advanced for the date of the
Crucifixion: while Pontius Pilate was procurator of Judea,
between AD 26 and 36, the Passover moon was eclipsed
only on the night of Friday–Saturday, Nisan 15, April 3–4,
AD 33.

Summary

Some biblical scholars may wish for a demonstration that the available data do not permit any year for the Crucifixion other than AD 33. To summarize the arguments, we first need to review the calendar differences of the period in order to appreciate the relationship between the two major New Years. Years in Palestine were counted from the autumn New Year according to the civil (Syro-Macedonian) calendar. The corresponding year in the ecclesiastical (Babylonian-Jewish) calendar began at the spring New Year which followed some six months later. This relationship is well known to have obtained in the Hellenistic (Hasmonean) period, but is unaccountably ignored by scholars studying the Roman (Herodian) period. We have seen (in Chapter 2) how this requirement, in conjunction with the coin evidence and the lunar eclipse (mentioned by Josephus) leads us to revise the date of Herod's death from 5 or 4 to 1 BC.

We can now summarize the principal data and arguments for the dating of the Crucifixion:

1. The Crucifixion occurred on the Day of Preparation of the Passover — Nisan 14 (John 19:14).

2. The Crucifixion occurred on the Day of Preparation of the Sabbath — Friday (John 19:31).

3. Pontius Pilate was procurator of Judea between AD 26 and 36 (Josephus and coin dates).

4. During the years of Pilate's rule, only Tiberius 16 (AD 30) and Tiberius 19 (AD 33) satisfy (1) and (2).

5. Since John mentions three Passovers during the ministry of Jesus, and the earliest possible Passover of the ministry is Tiberius 15, only Tiberius 19 remains as the year of the Crucifixion.

This analysis leaves us with Friday, Nisan 14, April 3, AD 33 as the only possible date of the Crucifixion. Working back from the date of the Crucifixion, this would place the Baptism in the Jordan some twenty-seven months earlier, in the month of Tebeth (January) AD 31. Luke tells us that Jesus was "about thirty years of age" when he started his ministry (3:23), which indicates that the date of the birth of Jesus of Nazareth was close to AD 1. Again we find strong correlation with our established date for the death of Herod the Great.

Conclusion

Nearly every book on the life of Christ includes a chrono-logical table and even a casual comparison reveals a wide divergence of opinion. For the historical date of the Nativity, writers ancient and modern have favoured each year between 12 BC and AD 9.

Largely governed by prevailing notions of the date of Herod the Great's death, the majority of scholars have placed the birth of Jesus in or before 4 BC. None of the Church Fathers dates the Nativity so early and the idea that Herod died as early as 4 BC seems to have been unfamiliar in early Christian times. J. Finegan[1] names early Christian sources as favouring dates between 4 BC and AD 1 (see Table 5, page 106).

However, when calendar, coin and astronomical data are taken into account, we established that Herod died early in 1 BC, soon after the lunar eclipse mentioned by Josephus, and probably on Shebat 2, January 28, 1 BC. This led us to a revision of the true dates of the Nativity events and a fresh look at the different accounts in Luke and Matthew.

Matthew's account is linked explicitly to the reign and death of Herod, with the story of the three wise men trav-elling from the East. We have described the probability that on their arrival in Herod's court the Magi proclaimed the opening of the Messianic Age which had been heralded by the triple conjunction of Saturn and Jupiter of 7 BC. Arriving in Jerusalem, they explained the Messianic signif-icance of the triple conjunction to the authorities there. On

Source	Date
Alogi (heretics)	4 BC
Irenaeus	4/3
Cassiodorus Senator	3
Clement of Alexandria	3/2
Tertullian	3/2
Origen	3/2
Africanus	3/2
Hippolytus of Rome	3/2
Hippolytus of Thebes (one fragment)	3/2
Eusebius	3/2
Epiphanius	2
Hippolytus of Thebes (another fragment)	2/1
Chronographer of the Year 354	AD 1

Table 5. Dates of the birth of Jesus in early Christian sources (after Finegan).

their journey which brought them finally to Bethlehem, the Magi would have followed the movement of Jupiter through the royal sign of Leo until Jupiter came to rest in Virgo at the beginning of January, 1 BC. At this time the Magi paid homage to the new-born son of the House of David.

In Table 6 we set out the conclusions reached when the differences between Matthew and Luke on the date of the Nativity are fully respected. Both Gospels are interpreted as dating the birth on Tebeth 9, but, as seen from the Table, twelve lunar months apart. This date corresponds to the

	Annunciation	Birth
Jesus (Matthew)	2 BC Nisan 1 April 6	1 BC Tebeth 9 January 6
John the Baptist	2 BC Tishri 1 October 1	1 BC Tammuz 9 June 30
Jesus (Luke)	1 BC Nisan 1 March 26	1 BC Tebeth 9 December 25

Table 6. Dates of the Nativities in Matthew and Luke.

western traditional Nativity date of December 25, celebrated in the Eastern Church on January 6, on account of the twelve day difference between the Gregorian and the Julian calendars.

Matthew and Luke's Gospels contain three annunciation stories and three corresponding births, all occurring in 1 BC. The Nativity story in Matthew, unmistakably relating the birth of a royal child, corresponds to the Eastern tradition of the January 6 birth-date — coinciding with the adoration of the Magi and followed by the Massacre of the Innocents — and occurs within the lifetime of Herod, before his death early in 1 BC. But the later date of December 25, 1 BC — identified in Western tradition — can be retained with respect to Luke's story of the birth of Jesus of Nazareth, after Herod's death. Jesus' birth would have taken place six lunar months after that of John the Baptist.

In an attempt to explain these three birth stories, the author has drawn attention to the traditional Messianic expectation of *three* individuals — the royal Messiah, the

Prophet, and the priestly Messiah. We find this expectation recently substantiated in the discovery of the Dead Sea Scrolls, the religious writings of the Jewish Essene order.

Up to the Baptism of Jesus of Nazareth (whose birth Luke alone narrates) all three Messianic figures are in some sense forerunners of the Christ Jesus. Then at the Baptism in the Jordan, all three Messianic roles are conferred on the central figure of Jesus of Nazareth: 'This is my beloved Son in whom I reveal myself.' (Matt.3:17) The mystery of the Incarnation is how these three roles, first associated with three distinct individuals, devolve on the single and unique person of Jesus of Nazareth.

On the basis of historical, biblical and astronomical research, we can reasonably conclude that the birth of Jesus of Nazareth seems firmly rooted in the year 1 BC. And since 1 BC and not AD 1 is the true year date of the birth of Jesus and the start of the Christian era, we can be pleased and satisfied with the timing chosen to celebrate the first year of the third millennium: namely the year 2000.

Appendix

Julian date	ERAS				REGNAL YEARS		
	Seleucid		Pom-peian (civil)	Actian	Emperor	Hasmon-ean	Herod *(civil)*
	civil	eccles		(civil)	(civil)	(eccl)	eccles
BC 70 spring		242					
70 autumn	243						
69 spring		243					
69 autumn	244						
68 spring		244					
68 autumn	245						
67 spring		245					
67 autumn	246						
66 spring		246					
66 autumn	247		1				
65 spring		247					
65 autumn	248		2				
64 spring		248					
64 autumn	249		3				
63 spring		249					
63 autumn	250		4				
62 spring		250					
62 autumn	251		5				
61 spring		251					
61 autumn	252		6				
BC 60 spring		252					
60 autumn	253		7				
59 spring		253					
59 autumn	254		8				
58 spring		254					
58 autumn	255		9				
57 spring		255					
57 autumn	256		10				
56 spring		256					
56 autumn	257		11				
55 spring		257					
55 autumn	258		12				
54 spring		258					
54 autumn	259		13				
53 spring		259					
53 autumn	260		14				
52 spring		260					
52 autumn	261		15				
51 spring		261					
BC 51 autumn	262		16				

Julian date	ERAS				REGNAL YEARS		
	Seleucid civil	Seleucid eccles	Caesarian (civil)	Actian (civil)	Emperor (civil)	Hasmonean ean (eccl)	Herod (civil) eccles
BC 50 spring		262					
50 autumn	263						
49 spring		263					
49 autumn	264		1				
48 spring		264					
48 autumn	265		2				
47 spring		265					
47 autumn	266		3				
46 spring		266					
46 autumn	267		4				
45 spring		267			Augustus		
45 autumn	268		5		1		
44 spring		268					
44 autumn	269		6		2		
43 spring		269					
43 autumn	270		7		3		
42 spring		270					
42 autumn	271		8		4		
41 spring		271					
41 autumn	272		9		5	Antigonus	
BC 40 spring		272				1	
40 autumn	273		10		6		*(1)*
39 spring		273				2	
39 autumn	274		11		7		*(2)*
38 spring		274				3	
38 autumn	275		12		8		*(3)*
37 spring		275				4	
37 autumn	276		13		9		*(4 =1)*
36 spring		276					1
36 autumn	277		14		10		
35 spring		277					2
35 autumn	278		15		11		
34 spring		278					3
34 autumn	279		16		12		
33 spring		279					4
33 autumn	280		17		13		
32 spring		280					5
32 autumn	281		18		14		
31 spring		281					6
31 autumn	282		19	1	15		7
BC 30 spring		282					
30 autumn	283		20	2	16		8
29 spring		283					
29 autumn	284		21	3	17		9
28 spring		284					
28 autumn	285		22	4	18		10
27 spring		285					
27 autumn	286		23	5	19		11
26 spring		286					
BC 26 autumn	287		24	6	20		

Julian date	Seleucid civil	Seleucid eccles	Caesarian (civil)	Actian (civil)	Emperor (civil)	Herod eccles	Herod's successors (civil)
		ERAS			**REGNAL YEARS**		
BC 25 spring		287			Augustus	12	
25 autumn	288		25	7	21		
24 spring		288				13	
24 autumn	289		26	8	22		
23 spring		289				14	
23 autumn	290		27	9	23		
22 spring		290				15	
22 autumn	291		28	10	24		
21 spring		291				16	
21 autumn	292		29	11	25		
BC 20 spring		292				17	
20 autumn	293		30	12	26		
19 spring		293				18	
19 autumn	294		31	13	27		
18 spring		294				19	
18 autumn	295		32	14	28		
17 spring		295				20	
17 autumn	296		33	15	29		
16 spring		296				21	
16 autumn	297		34	16	30		
15 spring		297				22	
15 autumn	298		35	17	31		
14 spring		298				23	
14 autumn	299		36	18	32		
13 spring		299				24	
13 autumn	300		37	19	33		
12 spring		300				25	
12 autumn	301		38	20	34		
11 spring		301				26	
11 autumn	302		39	21	35		
BC 10 spring		302				27	
10 autumn	303		40	22	36		
9 spring		303				28	
9 autumn	304		41	23	37		
8 spring		304				29	
8 autumn	305		42	24	38		
7 spring		305				30	
7 autumn	306		43	25	39		
6 spring		306				31	
6 autumn	307		44	26	40		Archelaus
5 spring		307				32	(8 years)
5 autumn	308		45	27	41		Antipas
4 spring		308				33	(43 years)
4 autumn	309		46	28	42		Philip
3 spring		309				34	(37 years)
3 autumn	310		47	29	43		1
2 spring		310				35	
2 autumn	311		48	30	44		2
1 spring		311					
BC 1 autumn	312		49	31	45		3

Julian date	ERAS				REGNAL YEARS		
	Seleucid		Caesar-ian	Actian	Emperor	Herod's successors	Roman Procurator
	civil	eccles	(civil)	(civil)	(civil)	(civil)	(civil)
AD 1 spring		312			Augustus		
1 autumn	313		50	32	46	4	
2 spring		313					
2 autumn	314		51	33	47	5	
3 spring		314					
3 autumn	315		52	34	48	6	
4 spring		315					
4 autumn	316		53	35	49	7	
5 spring		316					Coponius
5 autumn	317		54	36	50	8	1
6 spring		317			Archelaus dep.		
6 autumn	318		55	37	51	9	2
7 spring		318					
7 autumn	319		56	38	52	10	3
8 spring		319					Ambibulus
8 autumn	320		57	39	53	11	1
9 spring		320					
9 autumn	321		58	40	54	12	2
AD 10 spring		321					
10 autumn	322		59	41	55	13	3
11 spring		322					Annius Rufus
11 autumn	323		60	42	56	14	1
12 spring		323					
12 autumn	324		61	43	57	15	2
13 spring		324					
13 autumn	325		62	44	58	16	3
14 spring		325			Tiberius		
14 autumn	326		63	45	1	17	4
15 spring		326					Val.Gratus
15 autumn	327		64	46	2	18	1
16 spring		327					
16 autumn	328		65	47	3	19	2
17 spring		328					
17 autumn	329		66	48	4	20	3
18 spring		329					
18 autumn	330		67	49	5	21	4
19 spring		330					
19 autumn	331		68	50	6	22	5
AD 20 spring		331					
20 autumn	332		69	51	7	23	6
21 spring		332					
21 autumn	333		70	52	8	24	7
22 spring		333					
22 autumn	334		71	53	9	25	8
23 spring		334					
23 autumn	335		72	54	10	26	9
24 spring		335					
24 autumn	336		73	55	11	27	10
25 spring		336					
AD 25 autumn	337		74	56	12	28	11

Julian date	ERAS			REGNAL YEARS			
	Seleucid		Actian	Emperor	Herod's successors		Roman Procurator
	civil	eccles	(civil)	(civil)	(civil)	(civil)	(civil)
AD 26 spring		337		Tiberius			Pont. Pilate
26 autumn	338		57	13	29		1
27 spring		338					
27 autumn	339		58	14	30		2
28 spring		339					
28 autumn	340		59	15	31		3
29 spring		340					
29 autumn	341		60	16	32		4
AD 30 spring		341					
30 autumn	342		61	17	33		5
31 spring		342					
31 autumn	343		62	18	34		6
32 spring		343					
32 autumn	344		63	19	35		7
33 spring		344					
33 autumn	345		64	20	36		8
34 spring		345					
34 autumn	346		65	21	37		9
35 spring		346			Philip dies		10
35 autumn	347		66	22	38		
36 spring		347		Gaius		Agrippa	Marcellus
36 autumn	348		67	23=1	39	1	1
37 spring		348					
37 autumn	349		68	2	40	2	2
38 spring		349					
38 autumn	350		69	3	41	3	3
39 spring		350					
39 autumn	351		70	4	42	4	4
AD 40 spring		351		Claudius	Antipas dep.		Agrippa
40 autumn	352		71	1	43	5	= 5
41 spring		352					
41 autumn	353		72	2			6
42 spring		353					
42 autumn	354		73	3			7
43 spring		354					
43 autumn	355		74	4			8
44 spring		355					Casp. Fadus
44 autumn	356		75	5			1
45 spring		356					
45 autumn	357		76	6			2
AD 46 spring		357					

References

Ant. Josephus, *Jewish Antiquities*
War Josephus, *Jewish War*

Introduction
1 D. Wattenberg, Archenhold-Sternwarte, Berlin-Treptow 1969, 13.
2 *Ant.* 18.63f.
3 *Ant.* 20.200.
4 Tacitus, *Annals* 15.44.
5 *Ant.* 13.288–98.
6 Schalit, *World History,* Vol.6, 290f.
7 Schürer, *History,* II, 488ff.

1. Calendars and Festivals
1 Quoted by Finegan, *Handbook,* 37.
2 Finegan, *Handbook,* 37.
3 Olmstead, *Jesus in Light of History,* and 'Chronology of Jesus' life' in *Anglican Theological Review,* 1942. 24:3.
4 Eusebius, *Hist. Ch.* 32.16–19.
5 O. Pedersen, *Gregorian Reform,* p.19, quoting Josephus, *Ant.* 3.10.5.
6 O. Edwards, *Zeitschrift für die Alttestamentliche Wissenschaft,* 104/1, 1992.
7 Schaumberger, 'Die neue Seleukiden-Liste BM 35603 und die makkabäische Chronologie' in *Biblica,* 1955. 36:423–35.
8 Mishnah, Pesachim 5:1.
9 Goudoever, *Biblical Calendars,* 18f.
10 Goudoever, *Biblical Calendars,* 15.
11 Philo, *Decalogue.* 46f.

12 2 Chronicles 31:5.

13 Goudoever, *Biblical Calendars,* 45.

2. Herod the Great

1 *Ant.*15.373–76.

2 *War* 1.343.

3 *War* 1.343.

4 Meshorer, *Jewish Coins,* No. 30.

5 Meshorer, *Jewish Coins,* 66f.

6 A. Kindler, personal communication.

7 W.E. Filmer, 'The Chronology of the Reign of Herod the Great,' (in *Journal for Theological Studies,* 1966. 17.283–298); Edwards, *A New Chronology,* and 'Herodian Chronology;' Martin, *Birth of Christ;* Keresztes, *Imperial Rome;* David W. Beyer, 'Josephus Re-examined: Unraveling the 22nd year of Tiberius,' presentation to Society for Biblical Research, November 1995; and Finegan, *Handbook.*

8 *Assumption of Moses,* 6. Written *c.* AD 30. Editorial additions in brackets supplied by the translator R.H. Charles.

9 *Ant.* 17.167.

10 P.V. Neugebauer and R. Hiller, *Spezieller Kanon,* 46.

11 *Ant.*17.167.

12 *War* 1.33.6.

13 Thus E.L. Martin *(Birth of Christ,* p.53) quotes Burnaby: 'M. Moise Schwab, who studied the information about the scroll very intensively, felt that it was really the second of these, Shebat 2, that was the actual day which commemorated Herod's death.'

14 Schürer, *History,* 1.51.

15 *War* 2.183.

16 Finegan, *Handbook,* 301.

17 Burnett, A. 'The Coinage of King Agrippa I of Judaea and a New Coin of King Herod of Chalcis,' in *Mélanges.* Éditions NR, Wetteren, Belgium, 1987, 25–38.

3. Matthew's Nativity

1 Friedrich, 'Beobachtungen.'

2 Matt.16:22, Luke 18:34; 24:21, John 12:34.

3 Schürer, *History,* 2.503.

4 *Ant.*17.43ff.

5 Schürer, *History,* 2.506.

6 Virgil, *Fourth Eclogue,* 4–9. Translated in Brown, *Birth of Messiah,* 566.

7 1QS 9:11, Schürer, *History,* 2.550–54.

8 1QSa 2:11–22.

9 Kuhn, 'The Two Messiahs of Aaron and Israel,' in Stendahl, *Scrolls,* p.60.

10 Friedrich, 'Beobachtungen,' 265ff.

11 Eusebius, *Hist. Ch.* 1.3.10.

12 R. Steiner, *Gospel of Luke,* Ch.5.

13 *Ant.* 17.149–67.

14 Clement, *Misc.* 1.21.145.1–6.

15 Holzmeister, *Chronologia,* 43.

16 Ferrari d'Occhieppo, *Stern der Weisen.*

17 *see* Waerden, *Science Awakening II.*

18 Herodotus, *History* 7.37.

19 Censorinus, *De Die Natali.* 18.8.

20 Ovid (Pseudo-Ovidius), *De Vetula.* 3.595.

21 Bacon, *Opus Tertium,* 14.

22 B.L. van der Waerden in E.S. Kennedy, *Journal of American Oriental Society,* 1958. 78:259.

23 W. Burke-Gaffney 'Kepler and the Star of Bethlehem,' *Journal of the Royal Astronomical Society* 31, 1937, 417–425, explained the misconception as follows. Unfortunately, the author of an otherwise excellent chronological handbook (II, 406) published in 1825, Ludwig Ideler reported that a Danish Bishop Munter conceived the happy idea that the star followed by the Magi was none other than the conjunction of Saturn and Jupiter. Ideler, however, added that the hypothesis was not original but had been anticipated by Kepler. 'The prevalence of the error that Kepler held the Star of the Magi to be nothing but planets close together, is fundamentally due

to Ideler. His handbook which ran to a second edition in 1883, is much quoted; Kepler's work is little read.'

24 Roy A. Rosenberg delved into religious myth to explain the significance to the Magi of the conjunction. ('The "Star of the Messiah" reconsidered' in *Biblica,* 1972. 53:108).

25 Amos 5:26.

26 Martin, *Birth of Christ.*

4. Luke's Nativity

1 *Ant.* 17.174.

2 Beckwith, 'Christmas and the Priestly Courses at Qumran.' *Revue de Qumran.* 1977. 9 (1):73-94: 'Rabbi Jose said, "Fortunate things happen on a fortunate day, and evil things on an evil day. For as the first Temple was destroyed on a Sunday, the year after a sabbatical year, when the course of Jehoiarib was on duty, on Ab 9, so it was with the second Temple".' (p.82).

3 Early Christian writers sometimes treated Zechariah in an unwarranted fashion as the High Priest entering the Holy of Holies on the Day of Atonement, Tishri 10.

4 P. Winter in Schürer, *History,* 1.399–427.

5 *Ant.* 18.1–4.

6 Schürer, *History,* 1.381, and *Ant.* 17.271f.

7 *Ant.* 14.159.

8 *Ant.* 17.271f.

9 *Ant.* 17.288f.

10 *Ant.* 17.319f.

11 *Ant.* 17.228.

12 Schürer, *History,* 1.416.

13 *Ant.* 17.229.

14 Schürer, *History,* 1.399–427.

15 F.M. Heichelheim, 'Roman Syria' in Vol. 4 of Tenney Frank (Ed.) *An Economic Survey of Ancient Rome,* Hopkins, Baltimore 1938, 160ff.

16 Holzmeister, *Chronologia,* 41.

5. The Baptism of Jesus

1 Olmstead, *Jesus in Light of History,* 52f.
2 Levertoff & Goudge, 'Matthew' in Gore, *New Commentary,* 3.129.
3 Gaster, *Festivals,* 1.21–3.
4 Gaster, *Festivals.*
5 Girard, *Cadre chronologique,* 58.
6 Dionysius, *Paschate,* Arg.15.
7 Clement, *Misc.* 1.21.

6. The Crucifixion

1 John 2:13, 6:4 and 19:14.
2 Stauffer, *Jesus and His Story,* 66.
3 F.W. Farrer, *Life of Christ,* 1:22f.
4 Mann, *Bible as Read and Preached,* 288.
5 Guilding, *Fourth Gospel,* 125.
6 Edwards, *Time of Christ,* 137–40.
7 *Ant.* 18.35.
8 *Ant.* 18.89.
9 Meshorer, *Jewish Coins,* Nos. 229–31 respectively.
10 Philo, *Embassy to Gaius* 299–305.
11 Stauffer, *Jesu Gestalt,* 108f.
12 Humphreys & Waddington, 'Dating the Crucifixion' 745.
13 Curtius, 4.10 (39) 1.
14 Stephenson, 'The date of the Book of Joel' in *Vetus Testamentum,* 1969. 19:224.
15 Merezhkovsky, *Tod und Auferstehung,* quoted by Bock, *Caesars and Apostles,* 242.

Conclusion

1 Finegan, *Handbook,* 291.

Further reading

Abraham bar Hiyya Savasorda, *Megillat-ha-Magelleh.*

Africanus, The Extant Writings of Julius, Vol. 9 of *ANCL.*

ANCL. A. Roberts and J. Donaldson (Eds.) *Ante-Nicene Christian Library,* T & T Clark, Edinburgh 1867–1971.

Armstrong, A.H., and R.A. Markus, *Christian Faith and Greek Philosophy,* Darton, Longman & Todd London 1960.

Beyer, David W. 'Josephus Re-examined: Unraveling the 22nd year of Tiberius.' Presentation to Society for Biblical Research, November 1995.

Bickerman, E.J. *Chronology of the Ancient World,* Thames & Hudson, London 1968.

Bock, Emil, *Caesars and Apostles,* Floris Books, Edinburgh 1998.

Brown, Raymond E. *The Birth of the Messiah,* Chapman, London 1977.

Bruce, F.F. (Ed.) *Promise and Fulfilment,* T & T Clark, Edinburgh 1963.

Charlesworth, J.H. (Ed.) *The Old Testament Pseudoepigrapha,* Darton, Longman & Todd, London 1983.

Clement of Alexandria, *The Miscellanies,* Vol. 4 and 12 of *ANCL.*

Cullmann, Oscar, *Christ and Time,* SCM, London 1951.

Dead Sea Scrolls. English translation by Theodor H. Gaster, Secker & Warburg, London 1957.

Dionysius, *Liber de Paschate,* Migne. (Ed.) Vol. 67 of *Patrologiae.*

Edwards, Ormond, *A New Chronology of the Gospels,* Floris Books, London 1972.

—, 'Herodian Chronology' in *Palestine Exploration Quarterly,* 1982 (January–June): 29–42.

—, *The Time of Christ,* Floris Books, Edinburgh 1986.

Eusebius, *History of the Church,* Tr. G.A. Williamson, Penguin, Harmondsworth 1965.

Farrer, Frederick William, *The Life of Christ,* 2 vols. Cassell, London 1874.

Ferrari d'Occhieppo, K. *Der Stern der Weisen — Geschichte oder Legende,* 2 ed. Herold, Vienna 1977.

Finegan, J. *Handbook of Biblical Chronology,* 2 ed. Hendrickson, Mass. 1998.

Friedrich, Gerhard, 'Beobachtungen zur messianischen Hohepriestererwartung in den Synoptikern' in *Zeitschrift für Theologie und Kirche,* 1956. 53:265–311.

Gaster, Theodor H. *Festivals of the Jewish Year,* Sloane, New York 1952.

Girard, L. *Le cadre chronologique du ministère de Jésus,* Gabalda, Paris 1953.

Gore, C. (Ed.), *New Commentary on the Holy Scripture,* SPCK, London 1928.

Goudoever, J. van, *Biblical Calendars,* 2 ed. E.J. Brill, Leiden 1961.

Gray, John, *A History of Jerusalem,* Praeger, New York 1969.

Guilding, A. *The Fourth Gospel and Jewish Worship,* Clarendon, Oxford 1960.

Hennecke, Edgar, *New Testament Apocrypha,* 2 vols. SCM, London 1963–65.

Hippolytus. *Commentary on Daniel,* Vol. 6 of *ANCL.*

Hiyya, *see* Abraham bar Hiyya.

Holzmeister, Urbanus, *Chronologia Vitae Christi,* Scripta Pontificii Instituti Biblici, Rome 1933.

Hughes, D. *The Star of Bethlehem Mystery,* Dent, London 1979.

Humphreys, C.J., and W.G. Waddington, 'Dating the Crucifixion' in *Nature,* 1983, December 22/29. 306.743–46.

Josephus, Flavius, *Jewish Antiquities,* 7 vols. Loeb, Heinemann, London and Harvard University Press 1930–65.

— *The Jewish War,* 2 vols. Loeb, Heinemann, London and Harvard University Press 1927–28.

Kennedy, E.S., and D. Pingree, *The Astrological History of Masha'allah,* Harvard University Press 1971.

Keresztes, Paul, *Imperial Rome and the Christians,* Vol. 1, University Press of America, Maryland 1989.

Klausner, Joseph, *The Messianic Idea in Israel,* Allen & Unwin, London 1956.

Mann, J. *The Bible as Read and Preached in the Old Synagogue,* Vol. 1, 2 ed. Ktav, New York 1971.

Markus, R.A., *see* Armstrong, A.H. and R.A. Markus.

Martin, E.L. *The Birth of Christ Recalculated,* 2 ed. Foundation for Biblical Research, Pasadena, Calif., and Newcastle-upon-Tyne 1980.

Meshorer, Y. *Jewish Coins of the Second Temple Period,* Am Hasefer & Masada, Tel-Aviv 1967.

Neugebauer & R. Hiller, *Spezieller Kanon der Mondfinsternisse,* Astron. Abhandlungen (Ergänzungsheft) 1934. 9.2.

Occhieppo, K. Ferrari d', *see* Ferrari d'Occhieppo, K.

Olmstead, A.T. *Jesus in the Light of History,* Scribner's, New York 1942.

— 'The chronology of Jesus' life' in *Anglican Theological Review,* 1942. 24:3.

Ovid (Pseudo-Ovidius), *De Vetula.* Ed. Paul Klopsch, Leiden & Köln 1968.

Parker, R.A. and W.H. Dubberstein. *Babylonian Chronology 626 BC–AD 75.* 3 ed. Brown University Press, Providence, R.I. 1956.

Pedersen, Olaf, *Gregorian Reform,* Scripta Pontificii Instituti Biblici, Rome 1983.

Philo, Judaeus, *Decalogue,* Loeb, Heinemann, London and Harvard University Press 1937.

—, *The Embassy to Gaius,* Loeb, Heinemann, London and Harvard University Press 1972.

Riess, Florian, *Das Geburtsjahr Christi,* Freiburg 1880.

Schalit, Abraham (Ed.) *The World History of the Jews.* Vol. 6. *The Hellenistic Age,* Masada, Jerusalem 1972. Reprinted W.H. Allen, London 1976.

Schürer, Emil, *The History of the Jewish People in the Age of Jesus Christ,* 2 vols. T & T Clarke, Edinburgh 1973, 1979.

Stauffer, Ethelbert, *Jesu Gestalt und Geschichte,* Francke, Bern 1957.

—, *Jesus and His Story,* SCM, London 1960.

Steiner, Rudolf, *The Gospel of St Luke,* Steiner, London 1964 (Vol. 114 of complete works).

—, *Spiritual Guidance of Man and Humanity,* Anthroposophic, New York 1970 (Vol. 15 of complete works).

Stendahl, K. *The Scrolls of the New Testament,* SCM, London 1958.

Tacitus, *The Annals of Imperial Rome,* Tr. M. Grant, Penguin, Harmondsworth 1956.

Tuckermann, B. *Planetary, Lunar, and Solar Positions 601 BC to AD 1, and AD 2 to 1649,* American Philosophical Society, Philadelphia 1962.

Waddington, W.G. see Humphreys, C.J., and W.G. Waddington.

Waerden, B.L. van der, *Science Awakening II. The Birth of Astronomy,* Noordhoff, Leiden, and Oxford University Press, New York 1974.

Index

Abijah, priests' course of 72
Abraham 86
Actian era (AE) 24, 91
Actium 24
Adoration of the Magi 62
Agrippa I 49
Agrippa II 50
Alexander the Great 10, 100
Anatolius 22f
Antigonus Monophthalmus
    (Seleucid) 24
Antigonus, Mattathias (High
    Priest and King) 13, 35f, 40f
Antiochus III of Syria 11, 25, 37
Antipas, Herod (tetrarch of
    Galilee) 47, 76
Antipater (father of Herod) 37
Antiquities, Josephus 9, 45
Antony, Mark 13, 35f, 55
Archelaus (son of Herod) 47, 77
Aristobulus II 13
Assumption of Moses 44, 54
Atonement, Day of 84
Augustus, Emperor 37, 47, 61,
    74, 76

Baal 66
Babylon 10, 68
Babylonian Captivity 10, 32
Babylonian culture, religion 14,
    62
Bacon, Roger 64
baptism, rite of 84
— of Jesus 87
Bede, Venerable 7

Bethlehem 38, 58, 74
—, Star of 62–65
Brundisium, Treaty of 55
Burnett, A. 50

calendar 18–27
—, Gregorian 21
—, Hellenistic (civil) 26
—, Jewish 19, 21, 25–27
—, Julian 21
—, Palestinian civil 26
—, Syrian, Syro-Macedonian
    25f, 103
Caligula (Gaius Caesar) 42
Canaanite religion 66
celestial rhythms 19
census, Roman (enrolment) 71,
    73f, 78
Christ, birth of 61
Christmas 81
Chronicles, First Book of the 72
Church Fathers 105
Clement of Alexandria 61, 89
coin dating 42
coinage, victory 39
conjunction, Saturn & Jupiter 63
cosmic religion 63, 67
Crucifixion 91, 99, 101
Crucifixion, dating of 103
Cullmann, Oscar 25

Davidic king 54
Dead Sea Scrolls 53
Dedication, Feast of (Hanukkah)
    32

Dionysius Exiguus 7, 87f

eclipse, lunar 46, 59, 98
Egypt 58
Egypt, flight to 51
El, the high father-god of Canaan and Phoenicia 66
enrolment (of Luke's gospel) 71, 74f
Essene Order 53, 55, 83
Eusebius of Caesarea 57

Finegan, 105f
Friedrich, G. 53, 57

Gaius Caesar 78
Gospel chronology 18
Goudoever, J. van 30, 32
Gray, John 30
Great Conjunctions 63
Great Year 63
Gregorian calendar 21

Hanukkah (Feast of Dedication) 32
Harvest or Weeks (Pentecost) 27, 29
Hasmonean currency 41
Hebrews, Letter to the 57
Hellenistic or civil calendar 26
Heraclides Ponticus 67
Herod the Great 10, 13, 34, 37, 51, 60
—, reign 38
—, Jewish coronation 45
—, coin 43
—, court 105
—, last days 71
—, death 43, 71
Herod Antipas, *see* Antipas
Herod Agrippa 42
Herod Philip 49

Herodias 47
Herodotus 63
Hippolytus of Rome 80

Immanuel of Bethlehem 53
insurrection in Jerusalem 61
intercalation 22

Jerusalem 13, 18, 27, 32, 39, 41, 59
—, destruction of 74f
—, insurrection in 61
Jesus of Nazareth 53
—, nativity narratives and birth 38, 46, 56, 80
—, Baptism of 87
—, Luke's 58
—, Matthew's 56
Jewish calendar 19, 21, 25–27
Jewish month 19
Jewish War, Josephus 50
Joel 99
John the Baptist 18, 49, 53, 71f, 83
Jordan, River 84
Josephus 9, 23, 39, 42f, 45, 49, 59, 74, 76
Judaism, medieval 57
Judas Maccabeus 11
Judas the Galilean 74
Julian calendar 21
Julius Caesar 13, 21, 34
Jupiter 62f, 68

Kepler, Johannes 65
khamsin 101
Kronos (Greek god), *see* Saturn
Kuhn, Karl Georg 56

Leo (zodiacal sign) 68
Luke, Gospel of 49f, 58
—, Nativity 51, 71
lunar eclipse 46, 59, 98

Maccabean dynasty 35
Maccabean revolt 54
Magi 38, 51, 59, 63, 67, 105
Maimonides 19
Mariamme (wife of Herod)
    36f
Mark Antony 13, 35f, 55
Massacre of the Innocents 62
Mattathias Antigonus, *see*
    Antigonus
Mattathias the Hasmonaean 11
Matthew, Gospel of 51, 67
—, Nativity 56
Meshorer, Y. 41
Messiah, Messianism 53f, 57, 66,
    108
—, Royal 62
Mithraism 67

Nazareth 58
Nebuchadnezzar 32
new moon 19
New Year 18, 31
—, Jewish 86

Octavian (Caesar Augustus) 13,
    24, 35, 55
Olmstead, A.T. 22
Onias III (High Priest) 11
Ovid 63

Palestine 11, 25, 74, 103
Parthians 13
—, invasion 35
Passover 22, 27f
Paul, St 50
Pentecost (Whitsun) 29, 99, 100
Persian Wars 10
Pilate, Pontius 18, 96, 102
Pharisees 28
Philo 30
Platonists 67

Pompey 13, 24, 54
Prophet (awaited with Messiah)
    53, 55
Ptolemy 11

Quirinius (governor of Syria) 74,
    75
Qumran 53, 83

Resurrection 87
Revelation, Book of 57, 101
Riess, Florian 61

Sadducees 28
Salome 46, 49
Samaritans 28
Saturn 63, 66, 105
Schaumberger, J. 26
Seleucid era (SE) 24, 26
Seleucus (Alexander's general)
    11, 24
Sepphoris (in Galilee) 76
shepherds 51
Solomon, Psalms of 54
spring equinox 21
Star of Bethlehem 62f, 65
Steiner, Rudolf 58
sun, darkening of the 101

Tabernacles or Booths 27, 31
Tacitus 10
Tashlich (Jewish custom) 85
Temple (in Jerusalem) 28, 32,
    51, 59, 72, 102
Tiberius Caesar 18
time, 'linear' and 'cyclic' 25
Tycho Brahe 65

Van Goudoever, J. 30, 32
Varus (governor of Syria) 75f
vernal (spring) equinox 21
Virgil, *Fourth Eclogue* 55

Whitsun, *see* Pentecost

Xerxes 63

Yahweh 66
year 19
—, Babylonian 22
—, Great 63

—, Jewish ecclesiastical 22
—, Syro-Macedonian 26

Zealot movement 75
Zechariah 72
Zeus 66
Zoroaster, the 'Golden Star' 68
Zoroastrianism 63, 67